THE DRIVING FORCE

*Lessons in Teamwork
from Saturn and
Other Leading Companies*

THE DRIVING FORCE

*Lessons in Teamwork
from Saturn and
Other Leading Companies*

NANCY BROWN-JOHNSTON

Xephor Press

Xephor Press
3 Holly Hill Lane
Katonah, NY 10536
www.xephorpress.com
914-232-6708

ISBN 0-9752638-0-3

The Saturn Logo is a registered trademark of Saturn Corporation. While Saturn Corporation has granted authority to the author of this publication to display the Saturn Logo, Saturn Corporation does not endorse or assume any responsibility for this publication, the opinions expressed by the author, or the factual accuracy of any statements contained herein.

For international training and consulting services based on the concepts found in *The Driving Force*, contact Nancy Brown-Johnston at nbj@triplewin.info.

CONTENTS

DEDICATION

With love and appreciation for their support to my home team, Dean and Lindsey.

ACKNOWLEDGMENTS

THIS BOOK BEGAN AS MY PERSONAL PROJECT but blossomed into a full-fledged collaborative effort. I wanted to write about my experiences with teams yet knew the story would be richer if told with not just my own experiences but also with those of my global network of friends. I want to thank each person who submitted a story or a theory, helped with a reference, or encouraged me in this project. Although we are not famous authors or consultants, together we make up a contingent of successful practitioners that have supported team-based organizations in great companies such as Canadian Air, Chevrolet, Clark Equipment, Exxon Oil, General Motors, Harley-Davidson, Holden, Kellogg, Brown and Root, Office Depot, Opel, Saab, Saturn, and Shell Oil. Their willingness to team with me brought *The Driving Force* to life: Toby Andreassen, Carl E. Boyer, Frank Brilman, Gruffie Clough, George Gates, Goran Gorsson, Jan Honeyman, Sharon Johnson, Dean Johnston, Matt Kayhoe, Les Komanecky, Sharon Lambers, Joe LoCicero, Ellaine Long, Loey Lukens, Chuck Mallue, Brian McClelland, Shelley McLean, Guus Oosterop, Candy Pitcher, Ann Price-Perkins, Laura Plunkett, Karen Quay, Hans Reuser, Lori Robins, Debbie Rough, Sandy Sanders, Jane Sipe, Carol Talbot, Denny Teasdle, Wayne Townsend, Wayne Watts, and John Wiegand.

A special thank you goes to Deirdre MacDonald, from Scotland, who shared her research and dissertation information with me about Crew Management Teams, making the concept of quick-change teams clearer and more understandable.

The technical advice and editing from the Center for Effective Performance (CEP) and Xephor Press teams improved the readability and usefulness of this book. Special thanks to Suzanne Lawlor and Ruth Mills.

My gratitude extends to Saturn Corporation, General Motors, and Delphi Automotive Systems. I have been a proud employee, team member, manager, leader, and consultant in these organizations and have had many opportunities to learn and grow as a member and leader of all types of teams within the world's greatest companies.

After investing my entire professional life in working in and around teams, the time came to organize my thoughts and put key learning points to paper. Always the pragmatist, I made it my goal for readers to be able to use my work to help a team improve. I want teams to be a more respected and successful business strategy. I have used my membership and leadership experiences on natural work teams, project teams, virtual teams, quick-change teams, executive leadership teams, and global teams as the background for this book.

This project would have been impossible without the support of my family and cheerleaders: Joyce Brown, Linda Casale, Wayne and Beth Watts, and Fred and Michelle Brown. But when it all comes down to where I have learned the most about teamwork it is as a mother and wife. Special thanks to the members of my most important team, Dean Johnston and Lindsey Brown Johnston.

INTRODUCTION

THE DRIVING FORCE IS NOT JUST ANOTHER BOOK ABOUT TEAM-WORK THEORY. It is a guide to making teams, of all kinds and purposes, work. The benefits gained from reading this book are straightforward: learn from others who have done this work and who live with the results and discover simple, uncomplicated team-work tools that work. Competition is everywhere, and we are all looking for a competitive edge. The best strategy to long-term success is for every one of us to effectively leverage our own skills and those of other people to the fullest extent.

The approach I've used successfully at Saturn Corporation, General Motors, and in my consulting work is to leverage people through various types of teams. My approach to teams is to combine people's skills, talents, and interests to generate the maximum synergy, collaboration, and performance. This is not a new concept, but the room for improvement in the design and implementation of teams is tremendous. Many teams fail to reach their potential as measured by traditional performance measures. And many team members have less than positive team experiences. Teams need to be properly set up and then, once they are formed, must be maintained through a continuous improvement process.

I have been learning about teams and teamwork since the beginning of the 1960s. My education started with playing street football and has continued through all my school and work years. I played organized school sports, I studied small group theory, and I have witnessed the power of collaboration on the playing field and in the workplace. Teams became my life's work. In reality, teams are everywhere—in every part of life, in every industry, in every country. Done well, they motivate and teach us. Done poorly, they disappoint and inspire us to learn the lessons and not repeat the mistakes.

In the late 1970s, I facilitated the design and development of teams for greenfield and brownfield manufacturing plant locations and began working with teams in all types of industries. These numerous experiences helped me learn the hard way many of the lessons written in the thousands of books on teamwork. *The Driving Force* takes all of my lessons and helps you avoid the mistakes I and others have made with the simple goal of helping you do teams right! I want to improve the success rate of teams. I want to further our knowledge about teams. I want to help leaders, teams, and consultants "do teams better."

I frequently get asked—"How do teams work at Saturn?" *The Driving Force* is filled with responses to that and other teamwork questions. For example, at Saturn Corporation, the organization structure has always been built on teams. This is true from the working, operational level (where the vehicles are actually built) all the way to the strategic discussions at the top executive level. The project team that designed Saturn traveled the world and concluded that team-based organizations had the highest probability of success.

In 1987, when I joined Saturn, we weren't building cars yet, we were building the organization. My initial assignment included designing the assessment process to select employees who would make great team members, and creating the leadership selection process to identify team leaders who would succeed in growing self-managing teams. Once the team members and the leaders were selected, my job was to develop the skill sets of both the teams and the leaders through training, team building, and coaching. Working with teams taught me the real truths about conflict resolution, the importance of trust-building, and overall, the major role relationships play in all teams. The lessons I learned at Saturn and General Motors are described throughout this book, especially in chapters 4, 5, 7, and 9 on natural work teams, project teams, quick-change teams, and executive leadership teams.

I spent my first General Motors assignment in a greenfield, or start-up, participative management plant in Brookhaven, Mississippi. Designed in the mid-1970s, this plant began with a team structure, pay for knowledge, and job rotation, and its leaders were called "module advisors" instead of supervisors. To this day, the Delphi Packard Electric Brookhaven plant is benchmarked as a leader in team concept design. I was the internal training and organization development consultant, and the insight I gained in this first assignment has proved invaluable. It provides the basis for many of my own theories and beliefs about working in and with teams.

In the 1990s, my consulting and training work broadened to a global scope. I had the opportunity to work in Asia, Europe, and South America with executive teams and cross-functional teams. I witnessed the power and the challenges inherent in virtual teams and with global teams but also discovered the common truths about teamwork in any setting or condition. Some of the best new thinking captured in *The Driving Force* is on virtual and global teams.

In writing this book, I discovered an under-explored type of team that I have named *quick-change teams*. Quick-change teams are teams that have frequent changes in membership yet are expected to perform as teams. The goal is to not allow membership changes to interfere with reaching and maintaining high performance levels. The emerging opportunity is to capitalize on collaboration and teamwork in spite of changing membership. Quick-change teams challenge traditional team theory but are a reality in most large organizations. How to have successful teams in high change environments is the important and exciting topic explored in chapter 7.

Everyone will have their own favorite section of *The Driving Force* because it is written to reach a wide audience. It is written for people who have worked with all types of teams and had less than optimum results or for people who believe in teams but don't know where to begin. Whether you are a human resources specialist, a line-manager, an internal or external consultant, a coach, or a professor, this book was written with you in mind. It is also for people who want to improve their own experience as team members. With helpful things-to-do lists, user-friendly assessments, and the gamut of team types that are explored, everyone who is involved with teams can find useful ideas about what to do to improve their team experiences and overall success.

This book is also a collaborative effort from a global network of team practitioners and managers. It captures efforts that have worked in many types of teams in various work environments, and it presents a framework of how-to guidelines for team members and managers. It is written for you to take the chapters, tools, and ideas and put them right to work. The chapters capture real stories, answer important questions, and provide proven tools that can be used to diagnose your teams and then enable you to focus on the areas that need improvement. *The Driving Force* shares the approaches we have successfully used with teams to improve their performance. It is an integrated source of both theory and practical information in an easy-to-use format.

The book ranges from general information to specific activities. Whether your team is an executive leadership team charged with managing the entire enterprise; a natural work team tackling daily challenges; a problem-solving team brought together to focus on a specific, key organizational issue; or a virtual team that must work effectively together while working apart, there are ideas for you to use. The book also includes activities and assessments to make it easy to apply the concepts covered. It also outlines various experiential initiatives that have been used globally in a wide range of organizations. Finally, *The Driving Force* provides questions and checklists to help you address your team issues.

Examples of mistakes made with teams are all around us: in books, articles, and published case studies. *The Driving Force* shines an optimistic light on teamwork. The following chapters are about making teams work by understanding key lessons discovered in extensive work done with teams. These experiences have been documented to increase your own success with teams. Your first step is to find the chapter that best fits your needs and use the information to tackle the first challenge that comes to your mind. *The Driving Force* documents experiences from the "front line" by telling the stories of people who live there, work there, and learned about teamwork along the way. It then provides you with information and tools to increase your own success with teams.

Section I
Team Basics

CHAPTER 1

Making Teams a Good Business Strategy

TEAMS ARE A MEANS TO AN END, NOT AN END IN THEMSELVES. An organization decides to implement team-based structures for a variety of reasons. Some use teams as a basic building block to create operations that can innovate and respond flexibly to changes. Others see teamwork as a way to increase productivity, gain higher quality, or provide better service to their customers.[1] Some organizations create teams because they seem to be the best way to improve employee morale and increase loyalty and commitment. This is especially true if the organization espouses values of teamwork, trust, and respect for the individual—i.e., if it follows the credo that "people are our greatest asset." Whatever the reason for using teams, there is plenty to do to make them work. But when they work, the payoff is high—and it goes right to the organization's bottom line.

Suppose your ultimate goal is to increase your organization's effectiveness and profitability by increasing every team's

---

1. Katzenbach and Smith, *Wisdom of Teams*, 1993.

performance. The complexity of work, the speed of change, and the instability of organizations increase this challenge, but the payoff also increases when teams are successful. The investment to make a team "work" effectively is significant. To reap the benefits from using teams, an organization needs to make decisions about work distribution, training, compensation, manager and leader roles, and how power and control will be distributed. These are tough decisions that must be made. And linking team effectiveness to the bottom line is difficult to do.

When you can quantify the value of creativity, flexibility, and improved morale, you can quantify the contribution of teams. These are the most common payoffs gained from great teamwork. The more common measures are higher quality, increased productivity (schedule attainment), decreased absenteeism, or lower numbers of employee grievances. The intangible results of good teamwork are pride and excitement for the company and the products it produces. I have seen these results when teams are working, and I have seen the opposite results when, for a multitude of reasons, the teams and their leaders—and in fact, the entire organization—exist amid chaos. One great example is Saturn Corporation in the early 1990s. Saturn's teams were well trained, team membership had remained stable, and the level of organizational change was moderate. The teams met or exceeded their production schedules, they solved production problems effectively and quickly, they managed quality issues, and the organizational pride was evident by team members wearing logo clothing and driving Saturn cars.

Teams come in all sizes and are appropriate in a wide range of settings: on the factory floor, in the office, in the boardroom. Future chapters explore various types of teams and how each is unique, but some basic characteristics are true of all types of teams. The following lists ten key factors for evaluating the fit of using teams within organizations. The more factors that are operational within the organization, the more likely a team approach can work.

1. **Shared and flexible leadership roles:** The role of the leader shifts to the appropriate team member.

2. **Individual and mutual accountability:** Accountability is a promise and an obligation, both to yourself and to the people around you, to deliver specific, defined results[2].

3. **Interrelated performance measures:** Metrics connect team members to teams and teams to the overall organization.

4. **Open information sharing:** Information is available to make solid business decisions.

5. **Collaborative problem solving:** Problems are solved with a win-win approach.

6. **Shared commitment to goals:** Organization goals come before team and individual goals.

7. **Full use of individual members' knowledge:** The uniqueness of each team member is leveraged.

8. **Active participation in decision making:** Engagement and inclusion in appropriate types of decision making.

9. **Experimentation, innovation, and creativity:** Continuous improvement is expected and rewarded.

10. **Honest, trusting relationships:** A foundation of strong relationships is maintained.

How do you ensure that your team can perform and produce quality products and services? Once an organization embraces teams as part of its business structure, the answer to this question is that team building can enhance strong relationships and team skill development can improve individual teamwork skills.

---

2. Klatt, Murphy, and Irvine, *Accountability*, 1997.

Once the team is formed, your organization must set measures that reinforce the team's work, and you need to find skilled managers to guide that process. Implementing teams is an ongoing, time-consuming process.

For example, I recently downsized my training and consulting organization by 50 percent over an eighteen-month period. As part of the strategy to reduce resources while maintaining a high level of service, I reorganized the remaining twenty-five team members into three natural work teams. The results are fantastic. All ten of the factors listed above are in place. Team members have divided the responsibilities, become skilled in covering a broader range of responsibilities, and are managing the team tasks with great accountability. My role as team leader varies, from worker to coach to teacher to strategist—but mostly, I'm a coach. And I'm convinced that empowering team members to manage the increased workload got better results than any plan I could have created. All leaders have to be willing to allow for this participation to get great team results.

WHY BOTHER TO USE TEAMS?

Almost all organizations have experimented with teams. Early teams produced results and showed productivity gains while the level of work force commitment improved. Many companies removed levels of hierarchy, increased their managers' spans of control, integrated quality and production activities at lower organizational levels, combined operations, and opened up new career possibilities for workers in the 1960s and 1970s. When teams were successful, organizations saw gains in productivity, responsiveness, quality, and employee satisfaction. However, when the teams did not get the resources, training, and authority they needed, the teams never produced these benefits.[3]

In a team-based approach, job tasks are usually broadened to include aspects of team management with other, traditional job

---

3. Katzenbach and Smith, *Wisdom of Teams*, 1993.

responsibilities. Functions such as planning and problem solving are combined with operating duties. Teams are held accountable for their performance, and managers serve as resources instead of being merely supervisors. With management hierarchies relatively flat and with differences in status minimized, control and influence depends on relationships among the team members. Positional power is replaced with personal influence, and credibility is gained by building effective relationships. Success is tied to alignment, shared goals, and expertise, rather than formal positions on the company organization chart.

The right environment for teams is essential and is linked directly to building strong relationships. If an organization's culture uses an adversarial, win-lose approach, its teams will, too. Win-lose relationships do not result in teams being built. The best cultures for teamwork encourage *collaboration* and *partnership*, the outputs of win-win relationships.

TEAM SUCCESS IS ABOUT RELATIONSHIPS

Win-lose approaches ultimately curtail any true teamwork. To illustrate how important this is, consider the TripleWin Relationship Continuum shown on page 6. This model defines the appropriate relationships for creating and maintaining a team-based culture. On the far left, relationships are built on win-lose strategies. In this environment, teams, if they survive, usually do not reach high performance levels. In contrast, on the farthest right, relationships are built with win-win, collaborative strategies. In this environment, teams thrive and make strong contributions, generating a triple win—a win for the team member, a win for the team or organization, and ultimately, a win for the customer being served.

The continuum illustrates the desired state while recognizing the reality of win-lose organizations. Many organizations operate in an adversarial environment. Most of us have worked in adversarial situations—maybe we still do. The prevalent characteristics of such an environment are an "us versus them" mentality, blaming

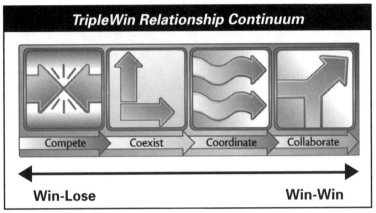

©TripleWin Consulting LLC, used with permission.

other people for problems, finding fault, and discouraging risk-taking. Let's take a look at each type of relationship shown on this continuum to better understand the problems facing teams in each type of organization.

Competition. In the negative extreme, team members use coercive tactics to compete within their own team to accomplish their personal goals. In this case, force and threats are used to control other team members. The strongest team members disregard the needs, rights, or feelings of other people on the team. Unhealthy competition results, and teams usually fail if these coercive relationships are not changed. Individuals openly challenge each other with a goal of making sure the opponent loses. Conflict occurs with such intensity that relationships are frequently damaged. In this approach, permanent damage to the success of the team and the organization can result. As individuals recognize that some of the things the team is doing do not benefit them personally, they challenge the team process and either leave the team or begin to clarify the boundaries of the team. The environment in the organization either encourages or discourages an adversarial manner of dealing with these predictable conflicts. If the team is going to survive, this combative style of conflict resolution must be replaced with a more collaborative approach. I watched this scenario play out when two training companies came to an end of their five-year agreement. Instead of finding the win-win, the discussion deteriorated into a legal battle that destroyed their relationship and ended all collaboration.

Coexistence. Along the way, people might decide to agree to disagree. This moves the team into coexistence, a type of team relationship that is still anchored in the win-lose environment and therefore drastically limits the team. Team members can be trying to work peacefully, but they have not yet started the open dialogue and debate that is required to get high levels of performance. The team is merely coasting. No one is really winning; people are merely playing not to lose. One approach is to go through the motions, say the right things, and maintain the appearance of teamwork but not really make the commitment to work at being a team. The dilemma is that this behavior interferes with true teamwork. This is often a comfortable place for some team members, but if it's left unchecked, the team ceases to grow. Coexistence is found in many marriages. Men and women allow their relationships to drift apart, fail to address conflicts and issues, and wake up one morning married to someone they don't feel they even know. As divorce rates demonstrate, coexistence often leads to a lose-lose result.

Coordination. When individuals decide to focus on a win-win approach to their work, the first relationship to form is one of cooperation and coordination. Teamwork begins. One person helps another person to accomplish his or her goal or task and begins to create a framework or foundation for teamwork. When team members develop cooperative types of relationships, they begin to work better together to coordinate their activities. They still see tasks as a specific person's responsibility, but they are willing to step in and help another person complete his or her task. The team members have started to work together, but they still have a long way to go to be truly successful and productive. Great examples of coordination are seen during times of crisis and natural disasters. During these times, personal agendas are put aside and people pull together to do what needs to be done.

Collaboration. The most effective level of team relationship is reached when team members develop shared goals and collaborate to accomplish them. Conflict is healthy because it brings new ideas to the table. People share ideas, resources, and responsibility. At this point, team members begin to work more closely together as they discover the interdependent aspects of their work. They agree to mutual team goals, and they find ways to achieve them as a team. They share information and knowledge to help each other be successful. Successful collaboration often leads to feelings of partnership. Commitment to the end result is evident. People approach situations without the baggage of competition, and they don't worry about other peoples' agendas because their goals are truly shared. The collaborative relationship is one of the strongest assets of a high-performance team. Team members trust each other, have common goals, and take responsibility for making sure every member of the team is successful so that the team as a whole is successful. The strength of collaboration can be seen in mergers of great companies. When both organizations bring their strengths to the new company and build a new way of doing business, the power of synergy is unleashed.

Improving Team Relationships

How a team moves along the TripleWin Relationship Continuum depends on the situation and the people involved. Getting to collaboration does not mean a team stays there, but it also does not mean that whenever anything negative happens, the team has to go back to win-lose. The goal is for the team to use a win-win approach to work out its problems and sustain strong relationships. This model guided Saturn Corporation, in its start-up, to involve people in the decisions that affected them. The payoff was shared ownership in the business and a commitment to meet business needs.

Under a team concept, performance expectations must define minimum standards and provide stretch objectives. Continuous improvement can be emphasized to reflect the requirements of the marketplace. Under all of the hard performance measures must be a foundation built on trust, respect, and mutual accountability. This is true for all types of teams.

THE CHALLENGES FACING ALL TEAMS

With all our knowledge about forming teams, why do so many teams crash and burn? This question and others must be answered to change the trend of failure of many team-based structures. The challenge for all teams is to function in a way that supports the organization's goals, to be aligned with the way works gets done, and to make a true, measurable impact on the business.

Another challenge is to address issues of low employee morale, quality catastrophes, productivity challenges, and increasing competitive pressures, without spending unaffordable amounts of money. When looking for answers, implementing a team-based structure often seems like a great solution. Theory and documented success stories[4] suggest that a team-based organization can generate extra energy from collective reasoning, or synergy. The dilemma is not usually found in the *forming* of the teams; instead, the dilemma is in setting up a team structure that is *aligned* with the company's culture and business strategies over the long term. Clear purpose gives definition, focus, and direction to a team. The purpose of a team then indicates appropriate allocation of resources. Without a meaningful purpose for having a team, all you have is a group of people trying to figure out why they are there and what they are expected to do. A team in this situation has little chance of being effective.

---

4. Larson and LaDasto, *Teamwork*, 1989.

> **"A PROSPECTIVE CLIENT ONCE ASKED,** 'can you come and
> do teams to us?' Wrong question. Besides the fact that no one
> can or should 'do teams to' any organization, the question
> misses the point: how and even whether to design and imple-
> ment the right kinds of workplace teams to fit an organization."
> — **George Gates, President, Core R.O.I. Inc.**

If the organization as a whole also lacks a clear sense of purpose, the work of a team is much more difficult. The team's purpose must be consistent and aligned with the organization's
mission. Making the investment to create a team structure includes clearly establishing boundaries of authority and responsibility, then investing in the development of skills in the areas of
decision making, conflict management, problem solving, and basic self-management.

> **"SUCCESS IN TEAMS INVOLVES A PLAN** of how the team will
> be managed, how decisions will be made, clear role clarifica-
> tion, conflict resolution process, clear team reward systems
> and norms. But ignoring the basic motivation of people will lay
> to ruin the best made plans."
> — **Carl Boyer, Retired Clark Equipment Manager**

Another key success factor is clear definition and development
of the role of the managers and supervisors who must support the
teams. Developing strong, effective leaders must occur simultaneously with developing strong, effective teams. In today's environment of rapid change, fast team development and fast
assimilation of new team members are more essential than ever
to a team's success.

Many successful and effective organizations do not use team-
based structures. However, an increasing number are discovering
the value of teams. Companies that successfully adopt team structures are clear about why they are implementing teams *before* they
implement them. They do their homework and invest the

necessary time, staff, energy, and organizational resources. They change the things that need to be changed to provide the correct environment or culture.

TEAM REALITIES

All over the world, organizations are discovering that with the right conditions, teams can be the right answer. In exploring the questions surrounding teams, many myths and assumptions must be clarified. Based on my years of experience, I have identified certain realities that cut across organization and country boundaries when it comes to successfully implementing a team structure. Therefore, I recommend that you examine these realities against what has gone on in your own organization and make the necessary adjustments.

Reality #1: More than 50 Percent of Major Change Initiatives Fail

As with any major investment, team initiatives succeed only when they are treated as seriously as acquiring a brand new business. This means providing sufficient up-front planning and resources and allotting sufficient time for growth. Teams are a *long-term* strategy that will only yield a reasonable return on investment over time. Statistics indicate that many team concept projects fail[5]. A combination of factors leads to this reality: poor planning, insufficient resource allocation, and ill-conceived implementation strategies are just a few of the more common mistakes. When an organization needs employees to actively co-manage the business and achieve higher quality levels or a stronger customer focus, a team-based structure can help. Teams only work when a framework to build and sustain the team is solidly in place.

Reality #2: Change Is Inevitable, and Every Change Causes a Team to Start Over

Even the best sport team starts over with a player change. When adding a new player, a team must step back, figure out what has

---

5. Hackman, *Groups That Work*, 1990.

changed, find a new rhythm, and establish a new game plan. This same premise holds true for work teams—and in today's rapidly changing business environment, a team that can make quick membership or task changes and accelerate the team's development is worth its weight in gold. Defining the change process, allowing for endings, making quick yet effective transitions, and moving on to strong, new beginnings is a formula for success[6]. Developing the mindset and the skills to allow a change to trigger an assessment of how things are going and to identify necessary changes is also key to the success of a team structure. When new members are added or a new and different task is handed to the team, the team must digress and start over in meeting its challenge. With skill and experience, this development process can happen quickly. Knowing the rate of change ahead, investing in team process skills that allow teams to become "quick-change" teams is a smart decision.

Reality #3: We Miss Opportunities to Learn with Every Team Failure
Every organization that has tried to implement a team concept has a tremendous amount of information about what worked and why, what failed and why, and what tools can be used to help teams in all stages, from start-up through continuous improvement. So why are we not getting smarter about how to implement and sustain teams? It may be that our organizations have a learning disability. As corporations try to do more work with less staff and fewer resources, the use of teams can provide more value than traditional business structures. This is true only if an organization has a process for capturing and using learning. Increasing the discipline in the set-up, implementation, and evaluation of all team initiatives would increase our learning. This requires the ability to think critically and implement proactively. It also may require organizations to admit when the team structures are not working. From that realization, decisions to repair, restructure, or regroup can save time, money, and wear and tear on the organization.

6. Bridges, *Managing Transitions*, 1991.

"WE TEND TO THINK OF TEAMS as having high-involvement norms, consensus decision making, and freedom to act, and we spend a lot of time training and developing around these elements. I've come to believe that instead we should focus on creating loyalty, ownership, and acceptance of the norms of the team. In teams, the motivation is 'What's in it for me?' This is not a selfish attitude; it's how the world works."

— **Carl Boyer, Retired Clark Equipment Manager**

Reality #4: Not Every Person Wants to Be on a Team

WIIFM—"What's In It For Me?" is a fair question. If the organization doesn't address individual employee concerns, it risks the success of the team initiative from its inception. You've all heard the clichéd adage that "there is no 'I' in teamwork," but many employees still feel that *I* do the work. Making assumptions about the nature of people and work may lead to problems down the road.

The key is to address each individual's concerns and questions. Is the team approach really meant to engage people in the business, and are people encouraged to work *with* as well as *for* each other? When this commitment is real, the organization indicates that it values and welcomes a diversity of opinion and approach. If the organization doesn't value and welcome such diversity, then it should tell people what to do with clear boundaries and expectations in order to yield better results. If an organization has decided a team structure is the right next step, skeptical members need time to evaluate their options. Most members of the organization will support the change. Those who do not must be provided a way to leave with their dignity intact.

"THE BEST TEAMS START FROM SCRATCH with a clear charter from above, resources to do the job, and the freedom to work and experiment. Each person had a way of contributing something unique and of value when they were working best. And they made a measurable impact on the business."

— **Chuck Mallue, Ex-Exxon Consultant and Manager**

Reality #5: Teams Are Not a Stand-Alone Answer; They Must Fit Clearly into an Overall Plan

Not every organization should implement a team-based structure. Teams do not work well unless the organization's structures and systems support them. They must reinforce the principles and values outlined in the company's vision and mission statement. A common question is "can teams work in a hierarchical structure?" The answer is maybe. In a hierarchy, teams must be a true extension of management, used to assist and support the needs of management[7]. If the organization can clearly define the purpose and roles of teams and set up mechanisms and structures to gain benefits, then teams can work.

If teams are not the right answer, having collaboration at the individual level can also lead to great results. Building trusting relationships, maintaining open lines of communication, and using teamwork to solve problems does not require a formal team structure to be in place. Equally important is what the organization recognizes and rewards. A quick way to undermine the success of the team structure is to reward individuals in a way that discourages them from helping other team members. Traditional systems, such as suggestion programs, ranking employees for pay raises, and individual performance appraisals, can subtly or directly communicate that teamwork is today's panacea, but individuals must really watch out for themselves. Without a strong foundation of congruent systems and structures, teams can easily fall apart under ordinary workplace pressures.

Reality #6: Most Organizations Haven't Figured Out the Manager's Role in a Team-Based Organization

Many managers struggle with the participative elements of team structures. Status has always been a privilege, even a goal, for management members. Leveling the positional power base requires an adjustment in thinking and a new definition of the manager's role. For managers at all levels, team-based management

---

7. Weisbord, *Productive Workplaces*, 1989.

can be threatening, and ignoring the situation does not make it go away. Failure to link managers to new roles that support and grow the teams is a big mistake.

To address the evolving role of managers within team-based structures, managers must become leaders, and as leaders they manage, provide strategic direction and operational advice, and build their teams. This is not only a way to deploy the managers, but this new role strengthens a team's performance by providing the right kind of management support. Unless the role of the managers is configured to include a role with the team, such as coach and team developer, the tension between the traditional approach and the team approach will render the organization ineffective. Teams rarely work if managers in the organization are unable or unwilling to inspire, empower, and support their decisions.

"THE TRUTH BEHIND MANY TEAM FAILURES is senior management. I can not count the times someone at a higher level has changed priorities, had his own idea instead, or just not had the confidence, guts, or skill to allow a team to flourish."
 — **Chuck Mallue, Ex-Exxon Consultant and Manager**

Reality #7: Achieving Team Effectiveness Is Not Cheap or Easy
What level of investment in teams leads to high performance? This is a good question, and one that needs to be answered when establishing teams. An organization must invest in training both team members and team managers. Skills in listening, assertiveness, conflict management, meeting management, problem solving, change management, creative thinking, and business basics are essential. In addition, training in team dynamics and team development is needed to prepare the team for the natural conflicts that will occur.

Ongoing opportunities for team building are also valuable. During team building, team members get to know each other, learn how to support each other, and determine the most effective ways to work together. This allows the team to form trusting relationships that help avoid pitfalls, wrong turns, and discouragement in the early stages of the team's development. With strong interpersonal and team skills, synergy and creativity can be unleashed and challenges can be dealt with as opportunities. However, team building is successful only if management continually reinforces the right behaviors after the initial creation of the team. Team development is an exercise regimen that must be followed *regularly* to maintain benefits. Thus, management support and attention are needed after the team is assigned as much as before.

Reality #8: It's Essential to Have Clear Accountability and Ways to Measure a Team's Success

What do companies hope to gain with teams? A popular saying is "what counts gets measured and what gets measured gets done." Therefore, a critical factor for teams is to have clear goals and performance targets. Every team must understand its goals, work toward them, and be rewarded when it meets those goals or suffer consequences when it misses them. Typically, goals would capture improvements in productivity, work processes, and quality. Additional benefits include flexibility to respond to situations and creative approaches to new challenges.

Once the goals are set, the team must be held accountable for its progress and be recognized for its accomplishments. A key to all teams, regardless of what stage of development the team is in, is to ensure there is sufficient discipline, alignment, accountability, and involvement in the team process. Then results and performance can be fairly measured. Without clear measures, teams falter and can become a hiding place for low performers and inefficiency. Unfortunately, poor performance can breed additional poor performance. When this occurs, it is not just a team problem, it becomes a leadership and organizational problem.

Reality #9: Teamwork Between Teams Is Difficult but Essential

Teams within an organization can disconnect from each other when they work in isolation. They may work on things that individually might be worthwhile but only contribute marginally to the *overall* performance of the organization. Synergy is missing. Sometimes, good individual team efforts end up at cross-purposes with each other. Too often, teams individually do worthwhile work, but collectively they go nowhere. This usually indicates the absence of internal strategies and systems that link teams and their individual missions into a larger collaborative purpose.

A better alternative is to find ways to link teams together. Having various teams working closely together creates an integrated organization. When teamwork is not integrated, the result is communication breakdowns and misunderstandings, and wasted time and work. The goal is to facilitate communication between groups and encourage the leaders to talk with each other and to strive to find connections and opportunities for teams to join forces and work together. As the saying goes:

TEAM = Together wE Accomplish More

There needs to be a *system* of teams, an interactive network of efforts that operate in synch toward common purposes.

CONCLUSION

Creating and sustaining high-performance teams is a formidable task. The formula for success is:

**Teamwork Values + Clear Goals + The Right Players
+ Skill Development + Team Processes
= High Performance**

By addressing each of these areas, an organization can create a foundation to implement teams that yield high levels of performance. Chapter 2 discusses each element of this formula for success. Then, the chapters that follow provide guidance to address all nine of the team realities introduced in this chapter and for successfully implementing the formula. As with people and organizations in general, every team is a unique mixture of people and opportunities. Yet even with the uniqueness of each team, the formula for success is a sound starting point.

CHAPTER 2

A Formula for Team Success

TEAMS ALLOW ORGANIZATIONS TO ENGAGE and involve non-managers in managing segments of the business. The philosophy is sound. Most of us believe that people support what they help create and appreciate having the ability to influence what happens to them. We also know that people bring more to the workplace than just their physical bodies. Most leaders also recognize that with business increasing in complexity, fully engaged workers are essential to deal with the constant changes. Frequent transitions are part of business survival.

Every team forms relationships, establishes roles, and faces times filled with conflict. Working through the conflicts provides the team with a reason to establish operating standards. In the beginning stages, a team must figure out who is on the team and what they are supposed to accomplish. Then, conflict and power struggles help the team surface issues and begin to define the team culture. After conflicts and disagreements, norms get established to clarify how the team will work together. By successfully navigating conflicts and disagreements, the team process is established and the team can focus on work and performing its tasks.[1]

When an organization implements teams, it's important for it to set the boundaries of influence and control. A hierarchy of teams with overlapping membership can serve multiple purposes. Saturn Corporation used such a hierarchy of teams, and it allowed for teams to work effectively in all levels of the organization. Besides timely information sharing, opportunities to leverage other teams' work can be quickly discovered.

As illustrated in the TripleWin Relationship Continuum model in chapter 1, encouraging coordination and collaborative partnerships shows support for teamwork. Internal competition and win-lose processes inhibit teamwork and must be replaced with win-win behaviors, such as honesty, effective problem solving, accountability, respectful relationships, and trustworthiness. Organizations whose value statements include respect for the individual, teamwork, and continuous improvement are indicating that they endorse a team-based culture. But the decisions and behaviors that operate the organization are the truer test.

Team structures must be endorsed through actions that are visible and consistent. A shared and clear vision can enable teams to be creative and innovative. Without direction, teams are useless. Therefore, the organization needs not only mission statements, philosophy statements, and lists of values; it also needs clear strategies and goals to assist teams in directing their activities. Connecting team goals to organizational goals enables teams to make meaningful contributions.

All of the key ingredients to successful teams are captured in the High-Performance Team formula:

**Teamwork Values + Clear Goals + The Right Players
+ Skill Development + Team Processes
= High Performance**

---

1. Tuckman, "Developmental Sequence," 384-399.

This chapter discusses in detail each component of this formula and recommends specific "things to do" to assure each component is fully implemented.

INSTILLING TEAMWORK VALUES

It is a paradox to describe values as part of an organization's foundation as well as part of the soft side of organizational development. Because no one intentionally builds a structure on a soft foundation, it is safe to conclude that there is nothing soft about clear, focused values. To determine if using a team approach is right for your organization, examine your true operating values. Values establish the work environment. The right values instill and reinforce a sense of pride, self-esteem, and shared responsibility where teams can flourish. Values are the fundamental beliefs that, when internalized, form the basis for organizationally acceptable behavior. That means everything else is out-of-bounds. Values consciously or unconsciously guide decisions and actions.

"TO BE A SUCCESSFUL LEADER in a team-based organization, you must do three basic things. First, clearly define the people, quality, schedule and cost goals. Second, give direction, resources, and support as needed. Third, allow your teams to run their own business; let them focus on the company as their business and not just yours."

— **Brian G. McClelland, Director,**
GM & Saturn Corporation

Teams involve people in decision making and problem solving beyond the traditional management circle. Successful teams have the right people doing the right things at the right time. To implement team practices, top leaders must trust and respect individual team members and believe in teamwork. Without a strong belief and true conviction that teams contribute more than individual performers, any adversity becomes reason enough to scrap the teams and put in place a more hierarchical, expert culture.

For example, Saturn Corporation's benchmarking studies uncovered the following common threads of successful companies[2]:

➤ Everyone shares ownership in the company.

➤ Equality is practiced, not simply preached.

➤ Communication barriers are eliminated.

➤ An open, trusting work environment exists.

➤ People are treated as the most important asset.

➤ Collaborative versus adversarial relationships are fostered.

➤ The focus is on quality as a top priority.

These threads link together to support a team concept. The core values and principles of high-involvement organizations must be congruent with the idea of employee involvement and shared responsibility for decision making. Moreover, reinforcement and practice keep these values alive. In reality, sometimes you fully live them and sometimes you do not, but committing to *try* is the right thing to do.

Having the right words is the first step, and committing to live them is the first real test. Figure 2-1 lists teamwork statements found in some major companies today. These examples serve as great conversation starters with top organizational leaders.

---

2. O'Toole, *Forming the Future*, 1996.

Figure 2-1: Corporate Mission Statement Examples

General Mills People will be the best in our industries—people who are winners, ever striving to exceed their past accomplishments. Exceptional performance is the result of these people working together in small and fluid teams on those issues where success will clearly widen our competitive advantage.

IBM Outstanding dedicated people make it all happen, particularly when they work together as a team.

Intel Great place to work: A productive and challenging work environment is key to our success. We strive to:
- Respect and trust each other
- Be open and direct
- Work as a team
- Maintain a safe workplace
- Recognize and reward accomplishments
- Be an asset to the community
- Have fun

Saturn TEAMWORK: We are dedicated to singleness of purpose through the effective involvement of members, suppliers, retailers, neighbors, investors, and all other stakeholders. A fundamental tenet of our philosophy is the belief that effective teams engage the talents of individual members while encouraging team growth.

Mary Kay Cosmetics Inc. Teamwork enhances performance because each individual contributes to the success of the organization where he or she is needed and appreciated by others.

Tom's of Maine We believe that different people bring different gifts and perspectives to the team and that a strong team is founded on a variety of gifts.

AT&T We encourage and reward both individual and team achievements. We freely join with colleagues across organizational boundaries to advance the interests of customers and shareowners. Our team spirit extends to being responsible and caring partners in the communities where we live and work.

Marriott Create an environment where all are empowered to care for customers and associates; an environment that is both enjoyable and productive, where each role or job is meaningful and important, where teamwork is the norm and pride is evident.

Levi Strauss Our work environment will be safe and productive and characterized by fair treatment, teamwork, open communication, personal accountability, and opportunities for growth and development.

Jones and Kahaner, 1995

Furthermore, as Saturn's benchmarking studies pointed out, we all know that values must be practiced, not just preached. So here are some things to do in your organization to ensure teamwork values are in place, are well understood by the members of the team, and are used to guide decision making.

Things to do to instill teamwork values:

1. Write values that simply and clearly explain the way the organization wants to operate.

2. Train the organization members in how to live by these values.

3. Always check key decisions against the values.

4. Do not significantly change the values once they are in place unless driven by a cultural change.

ESTABLISHING CLEAR GOALS

Shared, clear vision statements inspire creativity and innovation. Translating a vision into clear goals that can be implemented keeps teams from heading off with great intentions and ending up in the wrong place. Together, clear strategies and goals help teams organize, plan, and manage their activities. Most of us want to know that we are performing meaningful work. When we are part of a team with shared goals, the meaningful work is multiplied by the relationships we build.

Furthermore, no business can afford to waste resources. Organizations are continually forced to determine business priorities as they run out of time, people, or resources. Connecting team goals to organizational goals enables teams to make a meaningful contribution from the very beginning. It is a mistake to form teams that do not play an essential role in the organization.

Alignment to the organization's goals is critical. Teams often flounder when their priorities are unclear. They waste energy searching for direction from their leaders. When goals are missing, the focus shifts to being busy versus doing meaningful work. Looking busy can become the name of the game. The key is to convert goals into purposeful doing. The aim is to focus the energies and resources of the team on the right results.

Here are some simple, common rules of thumb for goal setting:

➤ *Write the team's goals down.* This makes the goals real. Over time, progress can be assessed and measured.

➤ *Involve the team in setting their goals.* People support what they help create. If I write the goal, I am more likely to remember it and be accountable to achieve it.

➤ *Make team goals measurable, specific, and achievable.* Use goals to direct the team's performance and motivate the right behaviors. Team members need to understand each goal and be able to quickly determine if and when they are making progress.

➤ *Assign deadlines to each team goal.* Without some form of deadline, patience and tolerance for nonperformance may slip into the team's approach. Accountability is a key component to high-performance teamwork.

➤ *Focus on performance goals.* All goals must be performance goals aimed at accomplishment rather than at good intentions. Linking team performance to organizational performance is key.

➤ *Balance goals to accomplish all priorities.* Goals have to balance all priorities. Balancing business needs with team member needs or long-term demands with short-term needs is never easy. Setting goals requires deciding where and when to take risks and striving for the right balance.

Unless vision and strategy are translated into understandable goals, teams struggle. Use goals to convert words into action. This is accomplished with a motivated group of people who understand

and commit to achieving a goal. Here are some things to do and some questions to answer to establish clear team goals within your organization.

Things to do to establish clear goals:

1. Establish and clarify the team charter.
   ("Why does our team exist?")

2. Define decision making and responsibility boundaries.
   ("What are the constraints and limitations?")

3. Establish open channels of communication.
   ("Who needs to know what?")

4. Clarify the team's and the team members' roles and responsibilities.
   ("Who is responsible for what?")

5. Maintain a customer focus in team goals and objectives.
   ("What do our customers need?")

6. State desired team outcomes in clear performance measures.
   ("How do we measure our performance?")

7. Link team strategies and goals to the key business or organizational priorities.
   ("What is our contribution to the bigger organization purpose?")

SELECTING THE RIGHT TEAM PLAYERS

The first question to ask each qualified candidate must be: "Do you want to work on this team?" If the answer is "yes," proceed. But if it's "no," say no thanks. Does that sound too harsh, a bit unrealistic, too naïve? Yet how can you create a high-performance team with people who do not want to be part of a team? Desire must be the price of admission to join the team; without motivated team players, the job of building a high-performance team is made significantly more difficult.

During the recruitment and selection process, discuss team-work values openly to ensure understanding and commitment. Get specific: link the philosophical aspect of values to concrete behaviors in order to remove dangerous ambiguity. For example, if confronting a fellow team member's nonperformance is going to be a responsibility of all team members, talk about that with each prospective member. If cross-training on all jobs is required, clearly explain that expectation. If this is a temporary assignment, discuss when and how the team members transition in and out of their current assignments. Ask potential team members if they can and will work fully in line with the team's values and the organization's values. If someone can not or will not, that person does not belong on the team. When possible, use your recruiting process to select people who want to be involved. Skills can be trained, but attitudes are tough to change.

The goal is to find the best people. Having great people makes motivating them easy. It also means spending less time handling problems or replacing people who don't work out. Success is assigning the right person to the right job. Selecting the wrong person is disastrous for everyone. Moreover, bear in mind that rigorous evaluation of candidates' skills and abilities takes time and skill. Be selective, and screen candidates primarily on attributes that are difficult to change through training, such as attitude, personality, and work ethic.

The above suggestions certainly work in a new hire situation when candidates are abundant and the jobs are desirable. However, there are times when the decision to form teams is made in an existing organization with people who may or may not think a team structure is a great idea. Teams can still work, and most of the principles are the same. Following is a checklist of recommended steps to gain both buy-in and commitment to help make teams work with existing organization members.

✔ **Checklist—How to Gain Buy-in and Commitment to Teams from Existing Employees**

✔ Discuss why teams are being formed (the business reasons).

✔ Involve people who have been on successful teams in the past.

✔ Find advocates and involve them early.

✔ Provide orientation and training on team concepts.

✔ Share how teams will work within the existing system.

✔ Outline the team processes that replace the individual processes.

✔ Define the duties of the team and its leaders.

✔ Sell the positives while remaining realistic to the challenges ahead.

✔ Hold meetings to have teams develop their norms.

✔ Provide time for teams to begin establishing effective working relationships.

✔ Keep team membership stable as long as possible.

✔ Have a method of de-selection that is consistent with organization values.

Having the right players allows a team to form and reach expected levels of performance. Using selection processes to guide this step can save hours of future problem solving and performance coaching of team members. Finally, consider the following ideas for selecting the right team players.

Things to do to select the right team players:

1. Be clear about what you are looking for by defining the duties of the technical, business, and team aspects of the job.

2. Determine attributes and characteristics that will help teams work.

3. Market the positions to attract the right people.

4. Use an assessment process that measures technical, business, and team skills and aptitudes.

5. Involve existing team members in the selection process.

6. Provide enough information so the wrong candidates will say no.

7. Provide orientation to the team concept prior to hiring.

8. Establish a probation period.

9. Have a de-selection process that allows people to leave with their dignity intact.

DEVELOPING KEY SKILLS

Training of the skills and processes used in a team structure should be ongoing and continuous. And the training should cover the gamut of technical job skills, business skills, and interpersonal skills.

Technical skill building ensures job readiness and quality output. Technical training must focus on the actual tasks the team performs (e.g., operating equipment, completing forms, producing reports, repairing machines, writing customer orders, etc.). With changing roles and technology, technical skills must match the tasks at hand. This makes the need for technical knowledge an ongoing, business-driven training challenge. Technical training is frequently a combination of formal classroom instruction and on-the-job practice.

Business training provides knowledge to make sound business decisions. In many organizations, some tasks are performed for employees by an administrative staff. But with self-managed teams, team members need to know how to perform these required administrative tasks (e.g., filling out time sheets, tracking quality performance, monitoring training hours, scheduling people, managing the budget, invoicing customers, etc.). Therefore, business task training must focus on how to fill out forms and follow procedures, ensuring the team knows what has to be done, how to do it, and who to go to for additional information or assistance.

Finally, *interpersonal skills* enable individual members to work collaboratively to make decisions, solve conflicts, address problems, and build effective relationships. Team members need to talk to each other, explain their points-of-view, agree or disagree about things, and eventually reach decisions on how to proceed. If a team cannot solve its own problems, it can't function as a team. An organization should develop a basic problem-solving approach that is understood and followed, in order to allow teams to work effectively. Interpersonal skills are essential and need as much consideration as business and technical skills.

Comprehensive training plans begin with adequate needs analysis and assessment. *Needs assessment* determines what people need to learn in addition to what they already know relative to the team's tasks. Assessment is the careful study of the context, job, skills, and knowledge that team members have or need before training is prescribed. The goal is to compare the desired skill level with the current skill level, factor in the individual and organization dynamics, and determine a training plan that yields optimal results.

Determining where to begin can be a challenge. The key to effective training is putting together a long-term plan that is comprehensive enough to meet both short- and long-term training needs and is flexible enough to change as the team or the organization changes. As teams become more knowledgeable and gain experience, they can determine their own training needs. The following checklist offers some important questions to answer in each of the three areas of skill development.

✔ ## Checklist—How to Develop the Team's Necessary Skills

Technical Skill Development

✔ What are the key technical skills team members need to master?

✔ What is the best way to assess current skill level?

✔ What training best provides this skill?

✔ Is the training available and affordable?

✔ If not, what are our other options?

✔ If yes, how can we best manage completing work while investing in necessary training?

Business Skill Development

✔ Which aspects of the business will the team manage?

✔ What processes must be followed?

✔ What are the key business skills team members need to master?

✔ What is the best way to assess current skill level?

✔ What training best provides this skill?

✔ Is the training available and affordable?

✔ If not, what are our other options?

✔ If yes, how can we best manage completing work while investing in necessary training?

Interpersonal and Team Skill Development

✔ What are the key interpersonal and team skills team members need to master?

✔ What team processes must be followed?

✔ What is the best way to assess current skill level?

✔ What training best provides this skill?

✔ Is the training available and affordable?

✔ If not, what are our other options?

✔ If yes, how can we best manage completing work while investing in necessary training?

Even with the best of intentions, training does not always receive the attention or priority it deserves. There are many reasons, some legitimate and some indicative of why so many team experiments fail. Figure 2-2 lists some common mistakes that organizations make. Watch out for these, and note how to correct them.

Figure 2-2: Common Mistakes Many Organizations Make in Developing Necessary Team Skills	
COMMON MISTAKES	**CORRECT ACTIONS**
Insufficient needs assessment	Take the time to understand the tasks being assigned to the team and to determine training needs.
Lack of true organizational commitment	Make the commitment to follow through and to give teams every chance to be successful—or do not begin.
Insufficient funding	Teams are not free; neither is the training and development they need, so establish an adequate plan and budget.
Insufficient training courses available	Buy, build, or borrow the right training.
Training conflicts with demand for work output	Establish a plan that protects time allocated for training.
Assume the people who were hired are totally skilled	Every person brings some skills to the assignment yet probably needs to gain additional information and skills to succeed in this new situation, so have realistic and adequate development strategies.
Training not applied on the job	Require adequate follow-up after training to ensure learning is applied and to measure training events' effectiveness.

Here are some things to do to develop the key technical, business, and interpersonal skills needed to build and support teams.

Things to do to develop key skills:

1. Conduct needs analysis in all technical, business, and interpersonal areas as part of the hiring step.

2. Create annual individual training and development plans to focus ongoing learning.

3. Consider the following topics when planning business, interpersonal, and team training:

Meeting Management	Listening
Problem Solving	Assertiveness
Project Management	Conflict Resolution
Creative Thinking	Feedback
Presentation Skills	Coaching
Budget Basics	Decision Making
Understanding Our Competitors	Eliminating Waste

DEVELOPING TEAM PROCESSES: FIVE CRITICAL ELEMENTS

Great teams do meaningful work. They spend their energy getting things done. They have a clear sense of purpose and are aligned to the organization's goals. The teams know they make a difference because they see how and where they make a contribution. Members make a personal investment and are valued for their contributions. To get these results, team processes need to be in place. Five critical team processes at the core or "heart" of successful teams include:

1. **H**onest dialogue

2. **E**ffective problem-solving and decision-making processes

3. **A**ccountability

4. **R**espectful relationships

5. **T**rustworthiness

Although there are other important aspects to team process, these five elements are essential in a team's early life. And although you want to honor everyone's individuality and encourage each person to make a unique contribution, you also need structure and guidelines to keep the team on track. Therefore, the following sections look briefly at each of these five critical team elements.

1. Honest Dialogue

For some teams, learning to talk to one another is a difficult aspect of the team process. Depending on the defined team responsibilities, this can involve a wide range of topics. Teaching a team to talk about issues in a timely manner is critical. Typical topics that should be discussed include:

➤ How to allocate work fairly among the team members

➤ How to allocate resources to the team

➤ Who will have which roles and responsibilities

➤ What norms or general principles of work behavior are necessary

➤ How to integrate new team members into the team

➤ How to evaluate team performance

➤ How to evaluate individual team member performance

➤ What business tasks (e.g., budget, scheduling, auditing, etc.) is the team responsible for performing

2. Effective Problem Solving and Decision Making

An organization solves hundreds, maybe thousands, of problems every day. Therefore, teams benefit by having a clear agreed-to process that allows work to be done efficiently and effectively, with high-quality decisions as the output. After solving so many problems independently, it can be difficult to involve other people in the problem-solving process—especially if they want to use a different process. Teams need to solve their problems rather than create additional ones. The goal of problem solving is intended to keep the team progressing while involving the right team members. Time must be spent to determine which decision-making and problem- solving processes the team will use. Common team decision-making processes include voting, majority rule, or a consensus decision-making process. Most processes can work if the guidelines are clear and the team supports them. A basic problem solving model is shown in figure 2-3. If this model is applied appropriately, it can provide adequate structure for the team.

Figure 2-3: Problem-solving Process

Consensus Decision-making Guidelines

➤ Appropriate team members gather to make the decision.

➤ All members of the team share facts, opinions, ideas, and feelings.

➤ Ideas are discussed to fully explore options and generate alternatives for the decision.

➤ The decision is written, and team members are asked if they are at least 70 percent comfortable.

➤ Everyone must reach 70 percent or higher comfort with the stated decision for it to become official.

➤ Everyone agrees to give 100 percent support to implementing the decision.

➤ All team members share accountability for supporting and implementing the decision.

3. Accountability

Teams need daily performance information. Feedback from customers must flow throughout the team to translate performance numbers into meaningful information. Teams that are held accountable for their progress and recognized for their output can manage their performance. All team members should know:

➤ What are the tasks belonging to this team?

➤ Who is responsible for what tasks?

➤ What is the leader's role within this team?

➤ How is the team rewarded for good work?

➤ What are the consequences for nonperformance?

➤ When there are performance or other team issues, what is the process for addressing them?

All teams need performance feedback from their managers. When their performance is good, it should be recognized and celebrated. When they miss targets, have a quality incident, or are over budget, having discussions about their performance and establishing action plans to get the team back on track send a clear message to all team members that they are accountable for their performance. As individual team members and collectively as a team, people need to know their roles and responsibilities. Then, they need to be trained, coached, and held accountable to effectively perform their work.

Team norms help establish the "field of play" for a team and establish the boundaries of accountability. A norm is simply the way people agree to behave personally and in interaction with each other. Stated norms say that the team will behave in a specific way, but the real and true norms are the team's observable behaviors. The purpose of norms is to:

➤ Clarify what is acceptable behavior within the team.

➤ Define how team members will treat each other.

➤ Define how business issues will be managed.

➤ Help maintain consistent behavior among members.

➤ Help maintain the team over time.

Typical norms include statements about:

➤ *Listening:* how the team makes sure everyone gets heard.

➤ *Information sharing:* how information gets shared from outside the team.

➤ *Decision making:* what decision process and what decisions belong to the team.

➤ *Conflict resolution:* how the team manages conflicts that come up.

➤ *Performance issues:* how poor performance gets addressed.

➤ *Responsibilities:* how work is assigned and who is responsible for what.

➤ *Meetings:* how often the team will meet and how it will manage its meetings.

➤ *Leadership roles:* what the team leaders' roles are.

➤ *Assignment:* how the team assigns tasks or positions.

4. Respectful Relationships

Strong teams are formed one relationship at a time. In the beginning, people tend to wait and see how another person acts. Then, something happens and a team member will see if he or she can trust other members of the team to do what is right. Then, after a while, people determine who they like and who they can trust. All events test our relationships, especially conflicts or tough problems to solve. The team will watch each other and form their long-term relationships based on the combination of all types of experiences. The team can become strong when tested if the character of each team member turns out to be strong and reliable.

The success of the team often depends on the values that were stated when the team was created and the consistency with which each team member adopts those values. The key word is often respect. Does each team member show respect for the rest of the team? Has every team member earned the respect of his or her teammates by his or her own actions? Without respect and team processes to handle conflicts and address performance issues, the relationships inside the team can be unstable and lead to significant performance difficulties.

Another key team dynamic occurs when team members change. Having a process to say good-bye and a process for assimilating new members helps initiate a relationship rebuilding process. In other words, a new member creates a new team. Time must be invested to allow the team to establish its new relationships and new team processes.

5. Trustworthiness

Trust is usually a product of time and experience. It needs all of the other key team elements we just reviewed—honest dialogue, effective processes, accountability to do what has been committed to, and strong, effective relationships based on respect. Trust is the basis of human relationships and does not always come naturally or easily. People must want it and work for it. But without trust, true teamwork is difficult if not impossible to obtain.

Trust-building characteristics and attitudes show up in every aspect of behavior[3]. Often it is how openly someone communicates their feelings and ideas. At other times it is demonstrated by showing support for the work of others. Or being willing to take risks and try new things. People make assessments all of the time about how authentic a person is and whether that person can be trusted in long-term, two-way relationships.

In the work setting, trust is built by focusing on solving problems and appreciating and accepting differences. How easily we work through conflicts, and how involved and how actively we work at our relationships—all influences how other team members view our trustworthiness.

---

3. Chartier, "Trust-Orientation Profile," 135-142.

CONCLUSION

Here are some final things to do to prepare an organization for teams.

> **Things to do to develop team processes:**
>
> 1. Add structure and guidelines to guide teams, not limit them.
> 2. Set the right parameters and boundaries.
> 3. Establish regular team meetings.
> 4. Determine a process to assess team effectiveness and schedule regular assessments.
> 5. Establish strong feedback systems to make information instantly available.
> 6. Link customers to the teams.
> 7. Display performance information.
> 8. Link compensation to performance.
> 9. Communicate and enforce consequences for non-performance.

One dose of information or training is not enough to sustain team growth and development. Ongoing development, combined with regular performance feedback and assessment, is critical. Information regarding what is working and what is not working must be part of the process. People recognize when things need to change. In fact, many of us get impatient when things do not change quickly enough or when they have not changed in the way we want them to. When things deteriorate or leaders fail to address obvious performance and accountability issues, the team effort is guaranteed to fail.

CHAPTER 3

Are You Ready for a Team?

BEFORE DIVING IN AND IMPLEMENTING TEAMS, it is wise to analyze how to get optimum business results. Done right, you can get quicker, better results with high levels of involvement and satisfaction for team members. Studies show that freedom, autonomy, and exciting challenges within a job are factors that motivate workers, but so are organizational practices that allow for involvement[1]. So, how can you figure out how a team structure can work for your organization?

The questionnaire in figure 3-1 can help determine your organization's level of readiness for implementing teams. The more "yes" answers, the more ready your organization is for teams. Where you answer "no," you should develop specific action plans to address the shortfall. This Organizational Readiness Assessment can be completed by individual managers and then tallied anonymously. Another option is to have the key management group work together on the assessments and reach agreements on next steps to address the areas needing improvement.

---

1. Lawler, *High-Involvement Management*, 1986.

Figure 3-1: Organizational Readiness Assessment: Are You Ready to Use Teams?

Directions: *This assessment is to be used to describe your organization using the listed organization practices as a guide. For each of the statements that follow, answer "yes" or "no."*

1. Are the organization's values aligned with implementing a team concept?

2. Do we pay attention to the organizational roadblocks that can interfere with the early success of teams?

3. Have we planned for changes and developed change strategies and skills?

4. Have we examined past change efforts, both successes and failures, and generated ideas to make sure this change initiative works?

5. Because teams are made up of people with their own individual needs and wants, are we prepared to address our team members' primary issues and concerns?

6. Will the team structure integrate into our daily operations?

7. Did we clearly link the team's purpose to the overall organization purpose?

8. Are the various teams connected together to assure alignment throughout the organization?

9. Can we provide clear, ongoing direction to the teams?

10. Have we comprehended the role of the managers in relation to the teams, and do we have a plan to train, reinforce, and continue to work with the managers in their new responsibilities?

11. Are sufficient funds and resources allocated to sustain the team effort once it is launched?

12. Is a method in place to hold teams accountable for a return on the investment?

```
Figure 3-1: Organizational Readiness Assessment:
Are You Ready to Use Teams?
```

Scoring

This Organizational Readiness Assessment can be completed by individual leaders and anonymously tallied. Another option is to have the key leadership group share their assessments to reach agreements about areas needing improvement and to identify next steps. Totaling the number of "yes" answers quantifies the overall level of readiness.

9-12 The organization has many of the characteristics required to support teams in place. Continue to monitor once teams are operational and reinforce effective practices.

5-8 Some of the key characteristics are in place, while others are missing. Teams are at risk in more than half of the required areas. Build on the organization's strengths, while addressing the missing areas. Teams are at some risk. For any "no" answers, develop an action item to address the shortfall.

0-4 Most or all of the characteristics are missing. Evaluate the potential for improvement, and establish a comprehensive development plan. If changes cannot be made, do not launch the team. For any "no" answers, develop an action item to address the shortfall.

If an organization cannot address the majority of the readiness areas, team success is at risk. However, once an organization has sufficient infrastructure in place to support teams, the next task is to determine which type of team best matches the business need.

CHOOSING THE BEST TYPE OF TEAM

Let's assume we have addressed the readiness issue and move to the next step, choosing the best type of team to accomplish the task at hand. Figure 3-2 summarizes the types of teams to consider, and chapters 4-9 go into more detail about each of these types of teams. The rest of this chapter provides an overview of all six team types and some things to look for in order to choose the best team for your particular situation.

Figure 3-2: Types of Teams			
Team Type	**Membership/ Purpose**	**Advantages/ Contributions**	**Common Challenges**
Natural Work Teams	Workers are assigned to a specific area to work daily on interdependent tasks with equal responsibility for the finished work. Typically, the members stay intact over an extended period of time.	• Shared understanding of the assigned tasks • Job enrichment through job rotation and expanded tasks • Increased flexibility • Sense of belonging	• Maintaining good relationships • Turnover of team members • Ongoing team development • Addressing poor performers • Team leader responsibilities • Cross-functional skills
Project Teams	Cross-functional representatives with various areas of expertise are assigned to solve a complex issue or problem.	• Creative solutions • Focused attention on the problem to be solved	• Gaining team cohesiveness • Turf or ego issues • Commitment to the team • Ineffective team processes

Figure 3-2: Types of Teams			
Team Type	**Membership/ Purpose**	**Advantages/ Contributions**	**Common Challenges**
Virtual Teams	Workers are assigned interdependent tasks but work from a variety of locations.	• Various individual needs and locations accommodated • Technology leveraged • Broader geographical area covered	• Maintaining team identity • Reliance on strong leader • Building team cohesiveness • Dependence on other's competence and performance • Understanding and support for goals and team mission • Resolving performance issues • Correct use of technology • Ineffective meetings
Quick-change Teams	Workers are assigned to a specific area to work daily on interdependent tasks with regular support from team leaders and managers.	• Team membership changes managed • New team members quickly assimilated	• Maintaining strong relationships • Conditional trust due to short-term experience • Reliance on strong leader • Turnover of team members

Figure 3-2: Types of Teams			
Team Type	**Membership/ Purpose**	**Advantages/ Contributions**	**Common Challenges**
Global Teams	Cross-functional and country-specific resources are assigned to a specific task: e.g., solve a complex issue that affects multiple country locations, create a process that works in a wide range of countries and cultures, address company issues that have cultural challenges.	• Creative solutions • Global focus • Shared understanding of issues • Diversity of approach • Involves multiple locations • Technology leveraged • Organizational alignment	• Cost of travel • Coordination of meetings and discussions • Gaining team cohesiveness • Ineffective team processes • Maintain team spirit • Addressing performance issues • Team leader effectiveness
Executive Leadership Teams	Senior executives reporting to a top leader are assigned overall operational and strategic leadership for the organization in addition to their functional responsibilities.	• Cross-functional decisions • Organizational alignment • Integration promoted • External environment focus • Tough problems dealt with	• Bias for operations versus strategy • Corporate policies • CEO must set clear direction to the team • Competition for promotions • Rugged individualism • Excessive homogeneity

Natural Work Teams

Natural work teams are a good choice when there is interdependence between the tasks and the employees. To organize into natural work teams, identify which tasks fit easily into a work module or segment. This is determined by grouping tasks that are either physically close, are sequential in nature, or require similar skills. Then, form the appropriate group of employees, ideally eight to nine, to complete the tasks with shared responsibility and accountability for the finished work. Typically the team members stay intact over an extended period of time.

The advantages of natural work teams include:

➤ Increased flexibility to make job assignments

➤ Increased ownership of the team tasks

➤ Higher organizational commitment of team members because of the sense of belonging to a team

The challenges that most natural work teams face include:

➤ Dealing with changing team membership

➤ Addressing poor individual team member performance

➤ Finding the time and resources to develop task and team skills

For many organizations, sorting out the role of the manager or supervisor versus that of the team is especially challenging. Chapter 4, on natural work teams, explores this challenge in detail.

Project Teams

Project teams are the right choice in a broad range of situations. They are used to solve all types of problems or to implement new programs or processes. Project teams work best when either cross-functional resources with various areas of expertise are needed to solve a complex issue or when a subset of the natural work team is assigned to tackle a team problem. A correctly formed project team can generate solutions by unleashing the creativity of the group that is brought together for a clearly defined assignment. By focusing attention on a problem and not being distracted by daily tasks to perform, problems can be solved faster than if they were left to the organization at large to address.

The advantages of project teams are:

➤ The solutions that a project team comes up with are usually creative and well reasoned, and they are owned by the people who are responsible for implementing them.

➤ A project team can focus better than ordinary employees doing their everyday jobs. Often, problems exist because it is difficult to find the time in our normal workday to focus on resolving the issues. A project team can be commissioned and directed to spend its time and attention on the specific problem and, in a specified amount of time, have a workable solution.

The challenges experienced by project teams include:

➤ Building the necessary team cohesiveness to get the necessary collaboration

➤ Having the necessary team process skills within the team

Sometimes the best answer is to assign external resources to provide the facilitation and group process skills.

Maybe the biggest challenge is keeping the project team connected to the rest of the organization so acceptance, commitment, and implementation of the proposed solutions are natural and easy. Egos and turf issues are the things to watch for in relation to long-term implementation. Having the buy-in at the launch of the project team, keeping key managers involved, and supplying information to the organization directly affected minimizes implementation issues. Chapter 5 details more of the keys to successful project teams.

Virtual Teams

Virtual teams can be a creative response to achieve teamwork when workers are assigned interdependent tasks but work from a variety of locations. Virtual teams require some level of interdependence, which provides the motivation for a dispersed group to work as a team. A second requirement is the ability of the players to occasionally meet face-to-face. This allows them to build strong relationships that can withstand the stress of long-distance relationships.

The reason virtual teams are worth the effort are the teamwork results achieved even when team members are in a variety of locations. Technology plays a key role in virtual teams by increasing the ability to connect people over a broad geographical area. Virtual teams face many challenges including:

➤ Maintaining team identity

➤ Building an ongoing team

➤ Staying connected and directed with minimal face-to-face contact

In addition, certainly one key to success is selecting virtual team members who have the personalities and skill sets to make this special type of team work. Chapter 6 provides guidance for selecting and maintaining virtual teams.

Quick-Change Teams

This is a new type of team that has developed in response to the perpetually changing organizations that still want to use teams to accomplish work. The quick-change team is a special kind of natural work team. What makes it special are workers assigned to a specific area to work on interdependent tasks, but their tasks or teammates change frequently. Because of the frequent team-membership changes, a quick-change team must be able to assimilate team members quickly. They cannot require extensive time to build strong relationships. Absolute keys to success are having team members skilled in group processes and having strong management resources to guide the team through any tough spots they encounter.

The main challenge to having successful quick-change teams is maintaining enough of a team environment amid high turnover and new personal relationships. This challenge and ideas for addressing it are covered in detail in chapter 7. Some team theorists believe that without stable team membership, a team cannot reach high performance. We need to deal with the changes: they are going to happen. Quick-change teams give us an opportunity to still get some of the benefits of teamwork. They require investment in each team member by building common and strong teamwork skill sets that can be put together with constantly changing members.

Global Teams

The globalization of many organizations has increased the necessity of global teams. In the past, organizations could solve problems, implement new programs or processes, and make decisions at the central office and could expect company-wide implementation of those solutions, programs, processes, and decisions. But this approach is rendered ineffective when a growing number of employees and customers are located outside of the country in which the company headquarters resides.

Global teams are a tremendous asset for either cross-functional problem solving or when a subset of the global workforce is assigned to tackle an organization-wide problem. A correctly formed global team can raise cultural issues and find solutions that have higher acceptance in the organization. Cultural problems can be identified sooner and addressed in the implementation plan.

Global teams can increase the consideration and sensitivity to cultural issues that interfere with implementation of a new process or procedure. The challenges experienced by global teams include:

➤ Building the team cohesiveness to get true collaboration

➤ Having the necessary process skills within the team

➤ Appreciating the diversity of approaches and opinions of the global team members

This last challenge is perhaps the biggest one: having the appreciation and the skills to leverage cultural diversity is an essential ingredient for any global team. Chapter 8 details more of the keys to successful global teams.

Executive Leadership Teams

In many organizations, forming the top management group into a team is a more effective way to manage complex organizations. The members of these teams are typically the top leaders and those reporting directly to them. The general purpose of executive leadership teams is to provide strategic direction and management of the entire enterprise. The advantages gained include cross-functional decision making and organizational alignment. These advantages are not achieved easily.

The challenges for the executives usually result from the following factors:

➤ The individualism of these top executives

➤ The approaches that help individuals earn these top posts

➤ The competitiveness encouraged, and even required as a top manager, may interfere with the collaboration and shared accountability needed in the executive leadership team

Although tough problems can be tackled and solved by the bright minds of the top leaders, the CEO must set clear direction and expectations in order to prevent individual performance from interfering with teamwork. More information on executive leadership teams is found in chapter 9.

CONCLUSION

There are basic skills required for any type of team. And there are areas to evaluate before implementing any team. Once these bases are covered, the next big decision is what type of team will best fit the situation. Six specific types are

➤ natural work teams

➤ project teams

➤ virtual teams

➤ quick-change teams

➤ global teams

➤ executive leadership teams

My personal experience with these types of teams is captured in the chapters that follow. And, like any person in the team business, I have learned as much from my failures as from my successes. I have seen great efforts end in failure because of inadequate long-term strategies or people issues. Or from major organization changes that destroyed the teams' foundation. I have also seen major problems solved and organization strategies developed with ease because of teams that work. I am convinced that teams with the right foundation can make a great contribution to any organization wise enough to use them properly.

Section II
Types of Teams

CHAPTER 4

Natural Work Teams

> **DEFINITION:** *A fully trained, interdependent group of people responsible for turning out a well-defined product or service. The team usually works together every day in the same work area.*

TEAMS COME IN ALL SHAPES AND SIZES. For many of us, the first team we experience is a sports team. Mine was on the Liberty Junior High School basketball team. To explore the important success factors for natural work teams, I returned to the basketball court and interviewed Ohio high school basketball coach, Wayne Watts. This interview, combined with my own personal experiences, surfaced seven critical elements of all natural work teams:

1. *Building the team:* creating a foundation

2. *Team leadership:* working team members, selected by peers, for a team leader role

3. *The coach's role:* handling the manager, advisor, supervisor, and team builder roles

4. *Sustaining the team:* handling daily challenges before they become problems

5. *Handling performance issues:* solving the inevitable problems

6. *Reinforcing the team:* building triple-win relationships—for the organization, the team, and individual team members

7. *Replacing team members:* making transitions

Once team members are selected, the challenge of blending individual styles, abilities, attitudes, and opinions into one unit is daunting. A balance between respecting and valuing what each individual brings with the rules of the team must be found. Without adequate structure, the team fails to form[1]. This chapter discusses the seven critical elements in detail.

An example of an effective natural work team was a human resource team that I experienced in my career. There were between twelve and sixteen members over the ten-year period of time. People came to the team because they wanted to do the work of the team. The leader had a philosophy about allowing people to make choices about their assignments, decisions, and actions and was committed to respecting every person's opinion and contribution. Members wanted input into the direction the team took, and the leader allowed for that shared leadership. Most members wanted a learning environment as well as a task one. That goal was accomplished with "stretch" assignments and the partnering of experienced and inexperienced team members. There was an expectation that members would collaborate and support one another and these behaviors were encouraged and recognized. As a result of their exceptional teamwork, this team's credibility and contribution were recognized throughout the company.

---

1. Larson and LaDasto, *Teamwork*, 1996.

BUILDING THE TEAM

"EACH PLAYER, FROM THE SMALLEST FRESHMAN TO THE MOST MATURE SENIOR, must feel an importance in being part of the family. The 'family' concept embodies so many of the behaviors we want our players to model that when roles are developed, the players are familiar with the concept as practiced in a family. Not everything goes right all the time, but when push comes to shove, we can all count on each other."

— **Wayne Watts, Basketball Coach, Hudson, Ohio**

A key to building the team is forming strong relationships. This begins with spending time talking and discussing but also doing. Working together is a great way for people to learn about each other. New teams need tasks to perform. After they have gained experience working together, the team has a framework for discussing how they can work together most effectively in the future. Theory is only useful when it helps deal with reality. Experience is the best driver of the team's operating norms.

Regular reinforcement and feedback are essential. Telling the team members how they are doing and what contribution they are making to their team establishes a connection. Once connected, people are inclined to actively participate and are motivated to make a contribution. During these regular communication sessions, coaching on areas to improve is natural and easier for the receiver to hear and accept. During open discussion and feedback sessions, managers can determine if the team has what it needs to be successful.

A team must have resources to perform its responsibilities. This can relate to budget, supplies, training, performance data, or even sufficient numbers of team members. Controlling team size is important. Teams of eight to nine members are usually an ideal size. In teams that have fewer than eight members, the opportunity for diversity and diverse opinions and the range of knowledge and experience decreases. Conversely, in teams with more than nine members, the opportunity to influence and play key team roles is limited. Again, the optimal size is determined by task complexity and level of task interaction.

A common mistake in team building occurs when organizing team-building events. Typically a team is taken away from the workplace, where the members spend hours in simulated team-building activities and discussion of possible learning points. Then they go back to work. But where is the connection to work? Without application of what they have learned, these teams will not reach a high performance level, and such "team building," for the most part, will be a waste of time.

In contrast to that approach, worthwhile team-building events include:

➤ Focusing on the team's needs by building on past team building, team strengths, and team needs

➤ Balancing fun, work simulations, and real work connections

➤ Focusing on skill building in the areas of communication, problem solving, and teamwork

➤ Building strong relationships among all team members

➤ Involving all key players: team members, team leaders, and coaches

➤ Matching the environment the team functions in every day

➤ Planning for follow-up (on-the-job) before the event is over

Follow-up and on-the-job application is critical to all team-building events. Teams are built one day at a time, one task at a time. Regular reinforcement and feedback are key tools. Plus, the daily work environment must allow teamwork to happen.

For example, the medical and safety team at Saturn went off-site to build stronger relationships among their group members.

The design of the session included get-to-know-you activities to facilitate personal disclosure among team members, teamwork activities to foster creative problem solving and breakthrough thinking, and then action planning to improve the overall functioning of the group. As a follow-up to this six-hour session, sub-teams were accountable for implementing the action plans and reviewing their progress at regular monthly meetings. This six-hour investment resulted in an overall improvement in camaraderie and everyday performance.

KEY LESSONS

FOR BUILDING EFFECTIVE TEAMS

➤ Strong relationships are not formed in one simple step. Early relationship building, reinforced with on-going team events and activities, creates the strong foundation needed for successful teamwork.

➤ Experience drives the team's norms. "One size does not fit all" because the personalities of the players establish the personality of the team. Within given boundaries, team norms evolve over time.

➤ An absence of boundaries results in dysfunction within the team. Clear definition of why a team exists and what the team is accountable to produce must be well articulated and understood.

➤ To ensure the team is set up to be successful, have a plan that includes training, sufficient resources, information, and time for the team members to do their work.

TEAM LEADERSHIP

**"ALTHOUGH NOT EVERYONE WANTS TO ACCEPT A LEADER-
SHIP ROLE,** successful teams have one or two strong players
who command respect from others, do everything that is
asked of them, and communicate effectively. The captains are
chosen by their teammates, so rarely are they considered the
coach's favorite. Successful leaders are those individuals who
have demonstrated the ability to be disciplined, selfless, and
empathetic."

— **Wayne Watts, Basketball Coach, Hudson, Ohio**

Most natural work teams select one or two team members to serve
as team leaders. Team leaders contribute to the team in a variety
of ways—as a working member, as a planner, as an administrator,
and as a link to the organization's infrastructure. Team leaders are
usually the primary interface with the manager, supervisor, or
coach assigned to the team. Team leaders handle operational issues and involve the external leaders or coaches when issues are
beyond their ability or resources. Methods for selecting team leaders range from careful assessment and structured interviews to
popular election. The issue therefore is often not how to select,
but what to do to ensure selected leaders are effective. The goal is
for team leaders to reflect and model the desired team member
behaviors. The first step to accomplishing this goal is defining
expectations for the team leader.

The role of a team leader includes being an effective team member. It is helpful for the team leader to be capable of performing,
even excelling in performing, the team's tasks. Developing subject matter expertise and contributing to the team's output are
ways a team leader adds value and gains credibility. However, in
addition to being a solid producer of product, the team leader
must also be a team *builder.*

Building the team includes assigning the appropriate people to tasks in order to maximize the team's output. Task assignments must comprehend both short- and long-term team requirements. Beyond daily production requirements, the team must also have adequate cross-training to ensure team flexibility. Balance again is a challenge. Production flexibility is important, but so is meeting daily performance goals.

A team leader must address performance and people issues before the overall team performance declines. When a team leader identifies a problem, works with the team to correct it, and implements a workable solution, the team gains maturity. The challenge is defining the problem and then selecting an effective approach to solve it.

✔ **Checklist: Basic Questions for Team Leaders to Ask**

✔ What is causing this problem?

✔ Who is involved?

✔ What effect is the situation having on the team?

✔ What is the most effective way to address the situation?

✔ What communications are required to keep the team informed?

✔ Who must be involved in solving the problem efficiently and effectively?

The ability to surface, or identify, and then solve problems is a sign of team effectiveness.

When the team is functioning at a high performance level, is when you know the team leader is succeeding. The overall goal is to provide the necessary leadership to integrate individual efforts and capabilities of team members into a high-performing unit.

KEY LESSONS

FOR DEVELOPING STRONG TEAM LEADERS

➤ Team leaders are selected by their teammates for a variety of reasons. Ongoing training and coaching are necessary to build strong leadership skills.

➤ Team leaders are role models. It is essential for team leaders to perform their work, complete their roles and responsibilities, and put the team's needs before their own.

THE COACH'S ROLE

"AS COACHES, WE PROVIDE EXPERIENCES IN THE PRE-SEASON that give potential team leaders a chance to step forward. The coaches and the captains work hard at grooming the team for a successful start. The coaches communicate with the players on a regular basis to remind them of their roles, to address any problems, to offer an opportunity to give input, and finally, and most importantly, to praise ANY positive behavior. Each player, from starter, high scorer, newspaper favorite to the twelfth kid that rarely plays, must know that completing his or her role is vital."

— Wayne Watts, Basketball Coach, Hudson, Ohio

The team coach is usually a manager or supervisory position. The coach role is to advise, monitor, direct, and teach the team without actually performing the work. The key to success is providing guidance to get results, while building the team's capability to perform as a high-performance team. A coach must know both the strengths and weaknesses of the team leader and each team member. This knowledge is gained by observing each person's level of competence in performing tasks along with his or her level of motivation and confidence. Then, the coach can select the right amount of direction and use targeted communication and instruction to promote the desired behaviors.

Staying engaged with the team is essential. Determining the right way to engage different team members is a challenge for most coaches. There is always an element of training or teaching involved in a coach's role. But there also is an element of empowerment, in which the team leader, the team as a whole, or a particular team member is expected to take the initiative and get the job done. It is the coach who directs when necessary and who turns over responsibility for decisions and implementation when appropriate. It is those actions that build a team. Ultimately, the key is finding a balance of *dependence, interdependence, and independence*[2].

The interaction between a coach and the team members comes during a series of events over a span of time. For the outcome of these interactions to be constructive, a strong relationship must be in place.

Here are some tips for coaches:

> ➤ *Have regular contact with team members* (initiate the contact; do not wait for a problem to arise; make contact your number one priority).

> ➤ *Respect each team member's time and opinions* (listen; ask questions; honor time commitments; create opportunities to discuss ideas).

> ➤ *Help the team solve its own problems* (avoid providing suggestions or solutions; help discover the facts; be a resource to find answers).

> ➤ *Grow the technical competence of all team members* (focus on helping them gain skills; discover how they learn; match teaching with ability to learn; encourage applied learning).

2. Covey, *The 7 Habits of Highly Effective People*, 1988.

➤ *Set goals* (clarify expectations; communicate minimum standards; provide performance feedback; challenge them to improve).

➤ *Multiply the team leader's effectiveness with your coaching* (differentiate the role of the team leader from the role of the coach; avoid doing the team leader's role; build a foundation for both roles).

KEY LESSONS

FOR TEAM COACHES

➤ Coaches need to establish and actively maintain strong relationships with their team members.

➤ The roles of the team leader and the coach need to be complementary yet differentiated and clearly understood to avoid role conflict.

Here is an example of an engineering team that failed due to poor coaching or leadership. The leader (coach) would not be specific about how the team was to operate and often had his own agenda. Changes did not get explained nor was team support sought. Members knew that if they could influence the leader privately, there was no need to work to get other team members to agree. Other members went around the leader to do their job. This team had low performance standards and inequity in opportunities from team member to team member. No drastic changes occurred until the leader retired and was replaced with a leader with a different style.

SUSTAINING THE TEAM

"AS THE SEASON PROGRESSES, COACHES COMMUNICATE WITH THE CAPTAINS on a regular basis to get feedback on the state of the team. The concept of sacrifice is essential to team success. Each player has to give up something. The process of changing "me" to "we" can take a long time, and there is no guarantee that if you reach it, it will stay with you for the duration. Once initial success has occurred, some individuals tend to start looking out for themselves (scoring average, name in the paper, etc.) and the bond that we have worked so hard to establish can quickly crash."

— Wayne Watts, Basketball Coach, Hudson, Ohio

Ask for feedback. Feedback is a great barometer for knowing how things are going and for determining where attention needs to be focused. It can come in a variety of formats, from a nod of the head to a detailed discussion. Whatever its form, feedback is valuable. Teams and team members need to receive constant, credible, and constructive feedback.

Ask the right people the right questions. To get useful responses, you must ask for the right information. The more focused your requests, the more helpful the information will be. Probe deeper when necessary to reach clear understanding. Consider complaints as gifts, as opportunities to address a concern before it grows into a major issue.

Here are some key components of giving effective feedback:

➤ Effective feedback focuses on behaviors, things a person can do something about, things that are within his or her control.

➤ Timing is everything. Picking the right time and the right location can set the best environment for the message to be heard.

➤ Specific information is usually more helpful than generalities. Specifics make it possible for the listener to understand exactly what the problem is and to develop a solution to correct it.

➤ Discuss one problem at a time to avoid information overload.

➤ Aim to help, not to hurt. The goal must be development, not punishment.

➤ Focus on the current situation rather than old issues.

➤ Consider the receiver's side of the story. Create a dialogue that results in everyone having a more complete understanding of the situation.

Feedback must be acted upon to be useful. So evaluate, consider, modify, change, or reaffirm. But do *something*.

Conflicts within a team can be resolved successfully. In conflict, we typically begin with the areas of disagreement. Switching the focus to find first what we agree on changes the tone of the discussion. Conflict occurs when the needs, interests, or wants of two people or groups are opposed to each other. It also occurs when two or more people attempt to meet different needs at the same time. It can occur when members of a team are closed minded to other options or when someone wants his or her own way in a group. Conflict is a fact of life.

In the context of a team, a successful conflict management tool is to find areas of agreement, and then use those points as a basis to resolve the inevitable differences. Today, the term "win-win" is commonly used. Although it may be challenging, finding a true win-win alternative builds a stronger team. Win-win reinforces that team members have shared responsibility for working toward an acceptable solution.

Successful resolution is a collaborative effort. Team leaders and coaches are responsible for helping teams work through their difficulties with a respectful and responsible process. Make the win-lose, me versus you, us versus them—in fact, any adversarial approach—out-of-bounds. Focus on *what* and not *who*. And establish deadlines for resolving the conflict!

Consider these points in planning your approach to any conflict:

➤ Conflict does not have to destroy relationships. In contrast, *avoiding* conflicts most often does.

➤ Facing conflict and resolving it can bring teams closer together.

➤ It is possible to resolve most conflicts. Some are just tougher than others.

➤ Conflict in itself is not bad. Neither are the people in conflict.

➤ No one needs to get hurt or lose to resolve most conflicts.

➤ Conflicts between team members and leaders are going to happen.

➤ Respect and good processes for talking through the differences are critical.

If you can approach conflicts realistically, you have a much better chance of resolving them constructively. Whether a conflict builds up the team or tears it down is almost totally determined by the way in which it is managed. When managed effectively, conflict actually becomes a source of energy and creativity in the team.

> **KEY LESSONS**

FOR SUSTAINING EFFECTIVE TEAMS

➤ Use feedback to determine what needs to be worked on. Healthy teams have open discussions about how things are going.

➤ Conflicts can bring about learning and growth. Left unmanaged, conflict can destroy even the most effective teams or coaches.

➤ Win-win solutions may take time to find, but they pay off big in the end.

HANDLING PERFORMANCE ISSUES

"**PLAYER FRUSTRATION, THE FORMATION OF CLIQUES, OR OTHER BEHAVIORS** that threaten the team bond must be addressed. The leadership of the team must take action before serious problems result. Using the captains and one-on-one conferences help."

— **Wayne Watts, Basketball Coach, Hudson, Ohio**

Close your eyes, maybe the performance issue will go away. Open them up, it is not only still there, it has probably gotten worse. The longer left unresolved, the more difficult a performance issue becomes to address. In fact, the issue may get bigger with every passing day. So, why avoid it? Begin by asking the following questions:

➤ What is the specific performance issue?

➤ How serious is the issue?

➤ What will happen if this issue is left unresolved?

➤ What is currently causing this performance issue?

➤ Are there past experiences that need to be explored?

➤ Who can best help identify solutions?

➤ What is the best first step to take?

To be effective, teams must exist in an environment that focuses on *getting results* rather than *finding fault*. If there is little or no room for error, there is little or no room for risk-taking. In a results-oriented environment, anything can be discussed with quick feedback and minimal defensiveness. This allows performance issues to be addressed without pain and suffering.

Treat performance issues as problems to be solved. The first action is finding the cause of the team member's unsatisfactory performance. Sometimes, the team member may see his or her performance as satisfactory, while the other members of the team consider it unsatisfactory. Objective data helps manage this disagreement by determining if the performance is actually good, marginal, or poor. Again, clear team standards or norms make this an easier discussion.

When performance is poor, answer this question, "What is the cause of the unsatisfactory performance?" Beware of assuming the nature of the cause. Here is a list of possible causes to consider:

➤ Unclear goals

➤ Personality clashes with other team members

➤ Personality clashes with the leader(s)

➤ Inappropriate job assignment or job description

➤ Lack of skills to perform the required task

➤ Insufficient time to learn new tasks

➤ Insufficient leadership direction

➤ Poor understanding of responsibilities

➤ Lack of motivation to perform tasks.

➤ Lack of commitment to the goals (laziness)

➤ Dissatisfaction with the job assignment

➤ Illness (physical, mental)

➤ Family problems

➤ Personal security concerns

➤ Job overload

Determining the correct cause or causes is certainly a critical step in the problem-solving process. If misdiagnosed, the problem will not go away, and attempts at solving it can frustrate everyone involved. Most leaders recognize the importance of setting their teams up for success. The leader must communicate to the team members precisely what is expected and what performance is required. It is critical, therefore, that each team member knows the following:

➤ Organizational requirements

➤ Specific assigned responsibilities

➤ Specific performance expectations

➤ Who to go to for support

➤ Measures to evaluate performance

➤ When and how performance information will be communicated

When the expectations are clear and relationships are strong, most performance issues can be addressed easily with positive results. Some situations, however, cannot be resolved; then individuals and leaders face tough choices. Removing a member from the team is a last resort, but one that must be taken if all other attempts at addressing poor performance fail.

KEY LESSONS

FOR HANDLING PERFORMANCE ISSUES

➤ Build an environment of trust and clear expectations so performance issues can be addressed with success.

➤ Performance issues get worse the longer they remain unresolved. Using good questions to determine the source of the problem allows leaders to address the right issues.

REINFORCING THE TEAM

"OUR PLAYERS ARE IMPORTANT AS PEOPLE AS WELL AS PLAYERS. We provide the opportunity for them to see us as people in addition to being their coaches. We can be together, we can enjoy each other's company, we can laugh together and form a stronger bond before we go to the gym. Then, when I really need to push them, to get in their face, to challenge them to give a greater effort, the players have those experiences to fall back on to cushion the immediate pain."

— **Wayne Watts, Basketball Coach, Hudson, Ohio**

Organization first, team second, individual third. That's the message team members must hear. Then, build on the individual and over time, the team is built and the organization succeeds. The key message is treat people right and they will do the right thing—most of the time.

Trust is a key factor. Trust defines itself in boundaries and restrictions. When high trust exists, wide boundaries and open information sharing are typical. Both the quantity and quality of communications increase. Trust levels fall across a continuum that we move along in our relationships. At one end is distrust, usually caused by previous experiences or lack of information. Narrow boundaries and controlled information sharing are evidence of distrust. Distrust often occurs when we do not know someone well or there has been a problem in our relationship. In a state of distrust, people figure out how to treat each other but protect themselves because they are not sure yet if they can trust. So they are careful. But a team cannot function well with a high level of distrust among members. Progress is slow, and the team will not get a lot accomplished.

The ability to trust someone is not always based on that person. It is often based on experience with other people. However, the experience with a specific individual is the most powerful part of building a trusting relationship. That is why opportunities to work together are critical to all teams. To reinforce the team, the team leader and coach need to actively address the issues that keep people from being able to trust one another.

The following actions help people increase their trust in their teammates:

➤ Seeing what other team members actually do

➤ Gaining experiences by working together

➤ Confronting inappropriate behaviors

➤ Having clear and serious consequences for violating the team's trust

Team structures must balance the needs of the individual with the needs of the team. Most people require an understanding of what they personally gain from working on the team (again, WIIFM or "what's in it for me?"). This is not necessarily out of a spirit of selfishness but out of a need to understand their place on the team. It brings to the surface the issue of personal motivation to belong to a team. The idea of winning together and losing together helps most teams stay aligned. Each person's role on the team, the contributions each makes, and the recognition each receives help team members stay motivated and actively engaged. It is through individual performance, collected through team accomplishment, that a team produces its results.

KEY LESSONS

FOR REINFORCING THE TEAM

➤ Balance the focus on the team and its individual members. It is not *one* of these, but *both* of these that generate the team's success.

➤ Provide opportunities to build trust. Address every incident of broken trust. Once trust is broken, it's tough to repair, but every effort must be made to do so.

➤ Practice trusting. Trust is both a noun and a verb. Learning to trust involves practice and risk-taking.

Here is an example of a team that didn't work and why it failed. There were eight members and no recognized leader. As a result, some team members were underutilized, the goals were unclear, and some individuals were treated better than others. Team members did not always step in and help other team members. In fact, it often seemed that the individual was more important than the team. The norms of the team were just on paper and not practiced in daily life. The stated team values were not taken seriously. Without leadership to correct the course of this team, it was disbanded after two years.

REPLACING TEAM MEMBERS

"IT ONLY TAKES ONE PLAYER TO NOT COMMIT to our team bond or to personally challenge the established leadership and the team's effectiveness is compromised."

— Wayne Watts, Basketball Coach, Hudson, Ohio

Every team member change is significant. Whether it is losing a team member or adding a new team member, the change creates a new team. Depending on the specifics, the ramifications can be small or large. The mistake is ignoring the change or failing to take time to rebuild the team. Of course, many factors contribute to this situation.

The first step to take is to say a proper and respectful good-bye to the member leaving the team. Taking time and finding a way to thank the departing member is important. It brings about closure and creates space for a new team member to enter. This may sound insignificant, unnecessary, or even silly, but team dynamics are often as strong as a family bond. Teams sometimes have to deal with grief and loyalty issues when they lose a team member.

The next issue is how to incorporate the new person into the team. Orientation to the team helps integrate and welcome the new team member. Reviewing team goals, norms, and performance to date helps that process. However, new challenges will occur that can only be addressed over time. Factors to consider in planning the entry of a new team member include:

➤ Providing time to grieve the loss of a valued team member. If the team was not close, adding a new team member might be a way to make the team stronger.

➤ Communicating the importance of maintaining high levels of results to the new team member. If performance needs to improve, discuss with the team how the new member will help improve performance.

➤ Showing appreciation and respect for the team's success. If the team frequently transitions team members in and out, make sure it does its usual good job at welcoming a new member.

➤ Maintaining a framework of yesterday's memories, today's reality, and tomorrow's challenges. Remind team members that *change is a key to growth.*

In any case, take the situation and make the best of it. When new team members are well integrated into the team, they bring energy and new ideas to the team. If not welcomed or oriented to the team, the team can lose time and enthusiasm. Allowing the new member to evolve into being not a new member, but just a member, is the goal. That comes with time and experience. Once the transition happens, all team members influence the team and find ways to make an individual contribution. All of the team processes come into play. It no longer has a new member; it is just a team, with members and issues and a certain level of performance. The goal is to take the team and help it be the best team it can be.

KEY LESSONS

FOR REPLACING TEAM MEMBERS

➤ Allow the team time and opportunity to say good-bye and thank you to departing team members.

➤ Spend time orienting new team members.

➤ Use adding or losing a team member as an opportunity to build a stronger team.

CONCLUSION

Organizations have difficult problems to solve in their day-to-day operations. Some organizations find forming natural work teams to be the best method to involve people in conducting daily business functions and operations. Teams of people who trust one another find the team environment a safe place to offer suggestions, make improvements, and take risks. With trust, everyone can take an active part in helping solve the wide range of problems that come up every day.

Natural work teams can solve tough operational problems through collaborative action. Natural work teams are simply teams of people who meet their team goals by working together. To achieve optimal performance from natural work teams, the top leaders and managers, along with the individual team members, must commit to following and supporting the team process. This commitment is fundamental. Without strong commitment, it is easy to walk away from the challenge presented by natural work teams.

Natural work teams can and do fail. They also can and do succeed. Success depends on spending sufficient time building the team, enabling effective team leadership, setting clear boundaries and accountability standards, handling performance issues, and doing regular team maintenance. Effective teamwork rarely happens without hard work—or the right people. Based on my work with natural work teams, I have identified eleven great team-player characteristics. They can be used to recruit, train, or even assess a team's health. I use the assessment in figure 4-1 as part of team skills training courses to have participants determine what areas they need to focus on to increase their own contribution to the team. There is power in self-examination and personal commitment to change.

Figure 4-1: Great Team Player Characteristics

Directions: *Read the following eleven characteristics, and rate yourself for how you act on* **this** *team.*

1 = poor   2 = okay   3 = great

_____ I communicate my feelings, opinions, thoughts, and ideas openly.

_____ I appreciate the skills of other team members.

_____ I help make well-informed decisions.

_____ I put the organization and team before my own goals.

_____ I help develop other team members.

_____ I honor the different opinions and characteristics of others.

_____ I care about other team members.

_____ I involve other team members appropriately.

_____ I build on the ideas of others.

_____ I do my share of the work.

_____ I listen to others.

Scoring

11-16   Room to make major changes. Your performance may be keeping the team from reaching high performance. Build on any "2's" or "3's" but select at least one of the items you marked with a "1" and make a serious effort to improve.

17-22   Identify items with a "1" rating and focus on improving your performance. Other team members may focus on your weaknesses versus your strengths unless they see you working on the low-scored items.

23-33   You are a good example to others. Keep improving your own performance while helping others work on improving their team behaviors.

Another important step in working with natural work teams is evaluating each team's effectiveness. Looking at the various aspects of the team provides insights into the dynamics that exist and quickly identifies which areas support, and which areas may interfere with, reaching high performance. The goal is to have a strong enough foundation to get high performance from your team. I suggest having teams complete the Team Effectiveness Assessment shown in figure 4-2 based on their existing or proposed team. Then, depending on the results, targeted work at improving team effectiveness can be tackled.

Figure 4-2: Team Effectiveness Assessment

Directions: *This assessment is to be used to describe your team using the listed characteristics. For each statement that follows, refer to the scale provided and decide which number corresponds to your level of agreement with the statement; then write that number in the blank to the left of the statement.*

1 = rarely   2 = sometimes   3 = often   4 = usually   5 = almost always

____ We have shared and flexible leadership roles.

____ We have individual and mutual accountability.

____ Our interdependent tasks and relationships are well understood.

____ We use measures that accurately track our performance.

____ We have open discussions and disclose all relevant information.

____ We use a collaborative problem-solving approach.

____ Our focus is on the production of actual products or services.

____ We have a shared commitment to our team goals.

____ Every team member's unique talents and knowledge is fully utilized.

____ We handle conflict in a constructive and direct manner.

____ Everyone actively participates in decision making.

____ We have agreed to established work procedures, and we follow them.

____ We have a strong group identity and perceive ourselves as a team.

____ We encourage reasonable experimentation, innovation, and creativity.

____ We maintain honest, trusting relationships.

Figure 4-2: Team Effectiveness Assessment

Scoring

The Team Effectiveness Assessment can be completed by each individual team member and tallied anonymously. Another option is to have team members share their assessments with the team at a team-building meeting to reach agreements about areas needing improvement and to identify next steps.

50-75   The team has many of the characteristics for high performance teamwork in place. Continue to monitor progress and reinforce effective practices.

25-49   Some of the key characteristics are in place, but others are missing. Build on the team's strengths, while addressing the low scoring characteristics.

15-24   Most of the necessary characteristics are missing. Evaluate the potential for improvement, and establish a comprehensive development plan. If changes cannot be made, consider disbanding the team.

CHAPTER 5

Project Teams

> **DEFINITION:** *A group of people, six to fifteen, often with cross-functional responsibilities, assigned to address a specified issue and recommend a course of action. The group disbands when the task is complete.*

I'VE BEEN A PART OF A LOT OF SUCCESSFUL PROJECT TEAMS. The best ones have been started from scratch with a clear charter from above, resources to do the job, and the freedom to work and experiment. Each person had a way of contributing something unique and of value when they were working best. And they made a measurable impact on the business.

A project team works best when people can see the direction they are going, see it as value added, and can get excited about it. A true entrepreneurial spirit exists, and everyone has a sense of ownership in the team's movement. People not only understand their roles, but also have interdependency and relationships with those around them. Having fun and making mistakes is encouraged. With a common value base solidly in place, trusting people can focus their energy on results rather than on process.

Project teams are not an antidote for poor product design, poor company strategy, or poor marketing. Yet project teams can help resolve these issues. The key is utilizing people with different skills and information to evaluate a situation and to generate creative, workable solutions. The time involved ranges from extensive efforts lasting over multiple months to four-hour meetings focused on tightly defined issues.

As with every type of team, project teams have unique circumstances that must be considered and addressed before the teams are commissioned. They must then be monitored throughout their existence. Whether they are commissioned to solve a small operational problem or to design an entire organization, all project teams or task forces must have the following critical success factors:

➤ The right group members motivated to perform the task at hand

➤ A clear definition of the problem to be solved

➤ A problem-solving process that matches the task

➤ Adequate group and meeting skills

➤ Ongoing leadership support

➤ A well-defined timeline

➤ Access to information and resources

➤ External resources, such as consultants or facilitators, to guide the process

The first part of this chapter explores each critical success factor, to clarify its importance to a project team's success. The second part of the chapter offers four case studies that illustrate how project teams work best.

CRITICAL SUCCESS FACTORS

The Right Group Members

Team size is definitely a factor. The right people are needed to generate the ideas, but group work is usually best performed by eight to nine people. The importance of a project team's work is symbolized by appointing key players to do the work. Once the team is commissioned, many practical items come into play. Questions like "when will we meet?" and "for how long?" are often the first to arise. The next issue to surface is often "who will perform my regular tasks while I am gone?" As with natural work teams, individuals assigned to project teams need assurance that their managers and the organization as a whole value their work with the project team. This can be demonstrated by allocating time for team members to perform the necessary project work without the burden and responsibility of having to complete their regular assignments.

Another unique aspect of project teams is the ability they provide the organization to assemble a group from across the organization, bringing a broad range of skills, experience, and perspectives to the task at hand. This diverse group composition allows for creative approaches, but the project team nevertheless needs to have a clear task, strong processes, and adequate meeting skills. If not carefully selected, the team members can have conflicting priorities that interfere with their task accomplishment.

A Clear Definition of the Problem to Be Solved

The commissioning leaders must set clear boundaries for tackling the task. Ambiguity is not helpful to project teams, especially in the beginning stages. Defining the "end in mind" and then commissioning the group to determine how to get there is a powerful approach. Regular progress checks by the sanctioning leaders can keep the group on track and encourage healthy dialogue. One major area to consider is how to handle controversial issues and ideas. In all organizations there are "sacred cows," those areas protected by senior people.[1] If the project team is expected to address these tough issues, it is essential to have that well defined and legitimized at the beginning, not somewhere in the middle of the project.

A Problem Solving Process that Matches the Task

Strong processes are essential in project teams. Even though most tasks take a basic problem-solving approach as described in chapter 2 (see especially figure 2-2), how to apply it to the task at hand requires careful consideration. Unique aspects may include researching other organizations, piloting a solution, or designing a new process that has never been tested. Addressing resource situations is the job of the sanctioning leaders. Adequate budget, time, and resources are always issues for project teams.

Adequate Group and Meeting Skills

As with other team efforts, team development and team performance issues frequently arise. Spending time early in the process forming intra-team relationships gives most project teams a strong beginning. In addition to spending time participating in team-building activities and obtaining team skill training, project teams must also spend time early on deciding the best approach to get their task done. Once leadership roles, power struggles, and team conflicts are experienced, the team is in a position to develop its own way of doing business. The quicker the team can get to work, the quicker team issues will surface. Once they surface, addressing them enables the team to determine how they can best work together. Without conflict, a team may fail to discover the best way to work together. The product of no debate or conflict is often uninspired or inferior solutions and recommendations.

Ongoing Leadership Support

Active demonstration of top leader support is essential throughout

---

1. Kriegel and Brandt, *Sacred Cows Make the Best Burgers*, 1996.

the time span of the project. In the beginning, the leader's key tasks are to help select the right players, clarify the task, set priorities, and provide encouragement. During the project, the leader should focus on providing guidance, encouragement, ideas, and sometimes supervision, and he or she may keep the group from stalling out or getting stuck in the middle of the task. Finally, at the conclusion of the project, the leader's commitment to make decisions quickly and to support timely implementation encourages participation and generates enthusiasm. Recognizing and rewarding successful project team members encourages future team participation.

A Well-Defined Timeline
Great work can be done in a short time frame if the right people are present, the task is reasonable, the resources are available, and leaders are committed. The timing of a task must be realistic with enough stress to keep the group moving. Progress reports and clear expectations regarding achieving stated goals enable a project team to monitor its progress.

Access to Information and Resources
To achieve breakthrough thinking, team members must be exposed to alternative ways of doing business and be given permission by their leaders to shatter the status quo, to evaluate and explore new alternatives. This can involve taking research or benchmarking trips, getting funding for experimentation, or even obtaining the necessary resources to pilot products or processes. Budget for this research needs to be planned at the beginning of the project team's work.

External Resources, Such as Consultants or Facilitators, to Guide the Process
Skilled process consultants can help the larger group and the subgroups accomplish their tasks in a timely manner. The role of these process "experts" must be clearly defined to avoid mistakes about the level of the team's dependence on these experts and

their involvement with the team as a whole. The overall goal of a project team is to do the work itself. The role of the consultant is to help the team with process issues so the team doesn't waste time and energy. The risk is that the team will become too much dependent on the consultant. A remedy for this is having one role of the consultant be to train the project team members on process skills, equipping them for future project team situations.

ORGANIZATIONAL READINESS FOR USING A PROJECT TEAM

The list of questions in figure 5-1 can help determine your organization's level of readiness for using a project team. The more "yes" answers, the more ready your organization is for a project team. For any "no" answer, you should develop a specific action plan to address the shortfall.

Figure 5-1: Project Team Readiness Assessment

Directions: *This assessment is to be used to describe your organization using the listed characteristics. For each of the statements that follow, answer "yes" or "no." For any "no" answer, develop an action item to address the shortfall.*

1. Have all of the right project team members been identified, recruited, and assigned to the task?
2. Are the project team members motivated to perform the task at hand?
3. Has a clear problem definition been written?
4. Has the problem-solving process that best matches the task been identified?
5. Do the project team members have adequate group and meeting skills?
6. Is a plan in place to train the project team?
7. Is a plan in place to assure ongoing leadership support?
8. Has a well-defined timeline been developed?
9. Have necessary approvals been obtained to ensure that the project team has access to necessary information and resources?
10. Have external resources, such as consultants or facilitators, been hired to guide the process?

CASE EXAMPLES

Project teams have been used successfully in many organizations. The following examples are stories of successful project teams. The first story represents an ongoing initiative, inspired by the events of 9/11, yet customized to fit a Southern state capital's need to address a wide range of city challenges. The second and third stories track major organization design projects from design to implementation. The second case study looks at the project team commissioned to design Saturn Corporation as a brand new car company—with new plants, products, people systems, and manufacturing processes[2]. The third case study tracks the design of the Delphi Automotive Systems plant in Brookhaven, Mississippi, from 1974 to today. This plant is widely recognized as an early success story of participative management. My findings also recognize it as an example of the effective use of project teams. The final example highlights General Motors' use of *GoFast!* project teams to quickly identify and address business challenges.

The diversity of these examples serves to illustrate the strength of project teams. Done right, they can assist organizations of every type and size in addressing challenges and generating effective action plans.

CASE STUDY #1

The Gateways and Cornerstone Initiative

This "Gateways and Cornerstones Initiative" was a U.S. city effort to prepare for an event that had visitors coming into town via Capital Street, a not-very-pretty experience. A plan was developed to clean up Capital Street—and keep it clean. The next phases would address other city gateways and cornerstones—sites where guests might visit an attraction. Neighborhood organizations were thought of as long-term partners with the government to help maintain the gateways. The mayor was inspired by New York City's handling of the September 11th tragedy and the partnerships that developed between New York's government and citizens.

To clean up the streets and the surrounding areas, all eight of the city's major departments were needed. For example, the fire department checked fire hydrants, houses for smoke alarms, and commercial buildings for proper exits and fire safety. The police issued tickets for abandoned cars and stopped illegal activities. A community improvement division of the city's planning department addressed zoning violations and abandoned houses, and the

---

2. LeFauve and Hax, "Managerial and Technological Innovations at Saturn Corporation," 8-19.

city's solid waste department cleaned the streets and ensured they stayed clean. The planning department also needed to work with neighborhood organizations so that they could be the ongoing eyes and ears of the project by helping prevent littering and by reporting crimes.

The deputy chief administrative officer was assigned the responsibility to develop the Gateways Initiative. She organized biweekly meetings with the departments involved to reinforce the message that the gateways were a priority. She also began developing a strategic plan to consistently address the issues in the gateways. This project team involved twenty interdepartmental representatives. The task groups agreed to meet twice a week and bring written reports of their department's accomplishments and plans for their Gateway activities.

Summing It Up: Results of the Project Team's Work

The group continued to meet twice a week. Some representatives brought in written reports while others simply related their progress. During the meetings, the attendees discussed accomplishments and concerns. The group was held together amid competing priorities by the knowledge that this was the mayor's initiative and that the deputy chief administrative officer represented the mayor. The group is now on its third gateway and maintains the first two gateways. Several issues have limited the group's progress:

➤ There is not a strong committee member focus on neighborhood involvement. The assigned person has not become fully involved.

➤ The team has not yet defined how progress will be measured. Identifying the measures and how they can be mapped to show the level of progress is one group's responsibility.

➤ A coordinator has been assigned to help keep the process moving but does not have experience in strategic planning.

Overall, this project team has shown the city office a new way to address working through bureaucracy, holding employees accountable to citizens, and collaborating with the community to achieve significant progress.

CASE STUDY #2

Designing Saturn Corporation

Is the work of a project team sustainable? To answer this question, I tracked the results of two project teams that were commissioned many years ago and then evaluated the state of the organizations they designed. In both cases, the majority of the proposed organization design was implemented and is still in place today. This is a testimony to the quality of the work the teams produced and indicates that task-force work has sustainability. The first of these cases is GM's creation of Saturn Corporation.

In 1981, General Motors (GM) was suffering from financial losses, a prolonged U.S. recession, and an escalating loss of market share of small-car sales to non-U.S. manufacturers. During this crisis, nearly 170,000 GM workers were laid off. Responding to this challenge, GM began to scrutinize both its products and its production process. While GM's Advanced Product and Design Team was designing a new small car, a second team was formed to design a new approach and organization that could successfully build a world-class quality car in the U.S.[3]

GM's industrial relations staff and the United Auto Workers (UAW) of the General Motors Department commissioned this second group to figure out a better way to do business. They began

---

3. O'Toole, *Forming the Future*, 1996.

with six people and then expanded to ninety-nine individuals to represent the collective knowledge of GM's plants and UAW locals. The task force was instructed to take a clean-sheet approach and propose the optimum way to integrate people and technology to manufacture small cars in the U. S. To tackle this challenge, the group organized into teams and set out to study different companies and processes around the globe. They studied the best of the best in terms of the processes used to manufacture vehicles.

Initially, the group came together for a week to prepare for taking a "clean sheet of paper" and creating a brand-new approach to building cars. The mission of the team and the philosophy of the future organization were used to explain the project's boundaries. During this orientation session, each of the ninety-nine members was assigned to one of seven teams. Each team was organized according to the engineering systems of an automobile and was assigned a process facilitator.

During the week, the small groups got to know each other and prepared for their part of the project. As part of their team building, they shared personal background information and agreed on operating norms for their group. At the conclusion of the orientation week, each of the subcommittees, ranging from six to fifteen members, developed a mission and philosophy that supported the overall group's mission and philosophy:

➤ **Mission:** Our mission is to explore ways to integrate people and technology to manufacture small cars in the United States.

➤ **Philosophy:** We believe that all people want to be involved in decisions that affect them, care about their jobs, take pride in their accomplishments, and want to share in the success of their efforts.

For two months, the teams visited forty-nine GM plants and sixty companies located throughout the world. Together they made more than 170 contacts, traveled approximately two million miles, and put in fifty thousand hours of study. Representatives from the subcommittees met periodically to communicate progress and resolve issues. The final report was an integration of the subcommittee reports, agreed to by the entire group during a final planning meeting.

During these fact-finding visits, the various subgroups observed and documented the practices in the most successful companies. These practices formed the foundation of the task team's final proposal. This proposal was reviewed and accepted unchanged by the commissioning executives. In January 1985, Saturn Corporation was born, the first new American car company in forty years. Saturn's task was to produce a small car that could compete with Japanese models. This was to be accomplished in a team-structured work environment as defined by "the Group of 99."

Summing It Up: Results of the Project Team's Work

Using a qualified consultant to guide the process and provide structure for the task force's proposal allowed this complex task to be shaped into a final proposal. Sub-grouping the ninety-nine team members into project teams that tackled a single aspect of the research allowed small-team success to blend into a larger whole. Integrating the small group proposals into one proposal was accomplished by weekly reviews of the group's work and having a common proposal template to follow. There was adequate support from top management and sufficient funding to do the necessary travel and benchmarking studies.

The group overcame several obstacles:

➤ They built strong subgroups by releasing task force members from their full-time jobs to participate on this study team.

➤ They enhanced cross-group communication with weekly reporting sessions.

➤ They involved team members who understood the problems of the current way of doing business.

➤ They stayed open to new ways of building cars by having a collaborative work environment.

Update

The Saturn Spring Hill, Tennessee plant implemented the concepts from the Group of 99 report, internally published as the Phase I and Phase II reports in 1987. A team structure continues as an integral aspect of the way Saturn operates, along with a co-management process involving union officials, management members, and Saturn team members. The foundation established by this task force work is in place today.

CASE STUDY #3

Designing the GM Packard Electric Brookhaven Plant (now part of Delphi Automotive Systems)

In the early 1970s, the final plans for a new plant in Brookhaven, Mississippi, were approved. The general manager saw this as an opportunity to change manufacturing practices and increase employee involvement. He commissioned a small group of seven highly skilled managers to design a participative plant structure. The members were high-potential young men who later became high-ranking executives. The group met with the general manager and was told that its assignment was to plan the operations for a new plant, but maybe most important, to come back with recommendations to the executive committee about how to *best* operate the plant. They had six months to complete their task.

The group was given complete freedom to decide the management structure, the roles of supervisors, and other production resources, along with any other related issues. The consultant asked for three days in some location away from the regular workplace for the initial meeting. This met with resistance from the group. The questions "What we would do for three days?" and

"Why couldn't we do that just as well in our plant conference room?" were foremost in the task force members' minds. Fortunately, the group finally agreed, and the group planned to begin its work with a three-day team-building and team skill-building event.

The first part of the meeting used typical team-building activities to help the group members get to know each other. It also helped the group determine how it would make decisions and handle conflicts among the team members. The second key aspect of the session concentrated on learning about new and innovative ways to manage people.

The task force studied innovative manufacturing projects. During this research, the members became more open to the idea of teams and gain sharing as possible business strategies. They also explored the needs and demands of the people who had a stake in this new plant—i.e., the employees, the community of Brookhaven, the management group back in the main Ohio operations, as well as the union officials who were not part of this endeavor. At the time of this task force, the plant was opening as nonunion.

As a final and key task, the group wrote a "Philosophy of Brookhaven" statement. This team effort resulted in statements that guided the decision-making not only for this task force but also for many individuals throughout the rest of their careers. Two key examples are:

➤ "People support what they help create."

➤ "Just as all employees are expected to contribute to the success of the business, they have the right to share in the benefits of that success."

The task force met about once a month for six months for two or three days at a time. In every case, they met away from the home plant. Each member had full-time regular assignments and this task was added on. With few exceptions, the task force members were able to get sufficient time away from the job. The final recommendations presented to the executive staff included:

➤ Replace traditional foremen positions with a management structure of "area advisors."

➤ Assign an implementation schedule along with responsibilities to manufacturing teams. The schedule would sequence team tasks from those most easily learned and accomplished to the most difficult, with an eighteen-month timeline for implementation.

➤ Create a proposal to organize manufacturing teams with team leaders selected by their peers. These team leaders would have specific duties that complemented the area advisor's role.

➤ Implement a "pay-for-knowledge" compensation system that bases wages on the number of different jobs a person could perform.

➤ Institute a profit-sharing system that shares plant profit with all organization members.

Summing It Up: Results of the Project Team's Work

Members of this project team credit the consultant for much of their success. He built the task force into a highly motivated team and prepared it for the job by providing relevant sources of information. He also provided excellent process guidance and a model for guiding the task force's proposal. A key success factor was appointing a team of bright, energetic people who quickly saw the potential of managing a plant in a new way and who became devoted to making a viable plan. The ongoing support of management, especially from the top of the organization, set this project up for success.

The group overcame several obstacles:

➤ Getting time away from their full-time jobs

➤ Breaking through corporate resistance for the concept of
pay-for-knowledge and gain sharing

Update

The Delphi Packard Electric Brookhaven plant continues to use
teams and the pay-for-knowledge system. It operates effectively
with strong employee relations and solid financial performance.
It has retained a philosophy of participation and trust in spite of
changes in leadership, products, and technology. The plant is recognized as one of the first successful participative unionized team
plant designs. It has been unionized since the early 1980s, and it
has the lowest number of grievances of any of the company's manufacturing plants.

CASE STUDY #4

General Motors' *GoFast!*

The previous examples illustrate the power of using project teams
to design organizations or to champion large change initiatives.
Another use of project teams is for tackling smaller, well-defined
issues in a short time frame. The most noted use of quick project
teams for problem solving is General Electric's Workout Process.
Jack Welch challenged his organization to break through bureaucracy and find ways to do more with fewer resources.[4] In 2000,
General Motors launched a similar initiative focused on fast problem solving and implementation of continuous improvement ideas.
The entire global enterprise has embraced this change initiative
under the name of *GoFast!*

The process is supported with process coaches, ongoing performance tracking, and recognition of success stories. The goal is
to move from structured project teams to *GoFast!* as the way of
doing everyday business. The *GoFast!* team members are both
salary and hourly employees throughout General Motors' global

4. Ulrich, Kerr, and Ashkenas, *The G.E. Work-Out*, 2002.

organization. Top managers champion the *GoFast!* workshops by defining the boundaries of the *GoFast!* team's task, identifying the right team members, and supporting the team's work from start to finish.

The agenda for the *GoFast!* sessions includes:

➤ "Leader kick-off message"—including the problem to be discussed

➤ Introduction of group members

➤ General description of the problem—i.e., defining what causes this problem and what aspects of this problem need to addressed

➤ Further definition of the problem—i.e., storyboarding topics that define the problem as a total group; identifying causes or key characteristics that must be explored

➤ Formation of small work teams—i.e., dividing the large group into break-out teams to work on a key aspect of the larger problem and to further describe:

  • Problem definition

  • Problem causes

  • Potential solutions

  • Recommendations, including action steps, owners, and timing

➤ Review progress with other groups

➤ Finalize recommendations

➤ Present recommendations to leader panel for decision

Success Factors

1. Having the right players in the room with a clear mandate allows the group to break through issues that have inhibited other attempts to address problems.

2. The top leader's presence and direction is essential.

3. Having strong facilitators assist in this sometimes emotion-laden process helps.

4. Having a well-defined process to follow, with clear desired outcomes, is essential.

5. Beginning with a clear task and ending with approved, well-defined action steps enable the group to make significant progress.

6. Progress occurs when individuals work through their concerns and issues and come up with agreed-to action steps as a team.

The obstacles to this process begin before the event. It takes time and top leader commitment and involvement to get the right players in the room. Another factor is the leader's confidence in the process. Once the players are recruited and present, the next goal is to ensure they are willing to accept organizational direction and make the right business decisions. Personal agendas must be placed aside, and teamwork must be accomplished. Without time to build teams, the challenge falls on the facilitator to manage group dynamics. Having people from different organizations working on tough issues with no time to develop relationships often leads to conflicts.

CONCLUSION

Project teams are suited for attacking issues that require special expertise from a range of individuals. They also work when the topic is either controversial or needs a wide base of support for implementation of the recommendations. Selecting the appropriate time frame for the work is as important as providing the resources and members to make up the project team. Not every problem can be solved quickly, and not every solution is obvious. Given the right players and the chance to work through the details, most project teams are a great investment.

Teaching key group skills to members of your organization is essential to problem solving effectiveness. The team must know how to handle conflict, manage meeting and member dynamics, follow a decision-making and problem-solving process, and make persuasive presentations. Without these skills, great ideas may never become much-needed solutions.

I have personally benefited from the work of the Saturn Group of 99 and the Brookhaven Task Force. I was a part of the implementation teams in both organizations. The work the project teams did in both cases established direction that lead to outstanding organizations. I am also a firm believer and advocate of the *GoFast!* process. My experience with *GoFast!* is that the project teams can use a targeted and straightforward problem-solving process to quickly solve business problems. The *GoFast!* initiative is the best organization development intervention I have used within General Motors. It gets the right people together, engages management, and monitors the implementation of approved recommendations. These aspects of project teams guarantee greater implementation of the required action steps.

CHAPTER 6

Virtual Teams

> **DEFINITION:** *A group of people working from a variety of geographical locations on interdependent tasks. Final output is a combination of individual and collective performance. Virtual teams can be either ongoing working teams or short-term project teams.*

PEOPLE WHO WORK TOGETHER AT THE SAME TIME AND PLACE ARE DECREASING IN NUMBERS. New organizations are often dispersed. Workers are employed in many different offices and locations and wear different hats. A company's employees no longer have to be in the same place at the same time to get the work done. Virtual organizations are forming in response to the global nature of organizations and business and the changing needs of workers and customers. A virtual organization is one that you do not necessarily see, certainly not all together in one place, but it nevertheless produces products or services. Growing technology capabilities and global business expansion help facilitate this change.

MANAGING TIME ZONES AND DISTANCE

Consider the experience of Jan Honeyman, Director, HR,

Infrastructure, for the engineering and construction group of Kellogg Brown and Root (KBR), the world's largest provider of products and services to oil and gas industries in the world. Jan serves as a member of a global HRD team because of geography. She is located in Australia, but her team spans Australia, the United States, the United Kingdom, Canada, Mexico, and Norway. She has two managers, one in Australia and another one in the UK. As with most virtual teams, the key to her team's success is building strong connections and communication systems.

"WHILE THIS WAS A STRANGE CONCEPT TO ME AT FIRST, I am now getting used to it. We are in regular e-mail contact (probably every second day) and have formal teleconference meetings once a month and informal ones usually during the month. Our virtual team seems to work quite well, although there are difficulties in understanding accents, and the telephone lag combined with speaker phones seem to work against us! The entire team is patient and tolerant, and this undoubtedly helps it all work. In addition, we also have a team Web site on our intranet so that we can share documents, course outlines, presentations, and anything else we find useful. This is a new idea for us, but it sounds like it will be really useful. As well as rotating which country we will meet in, our teleconferences are also planned so that we share the inconvenience!"

— **Jan Honeyman, Director, HR, Infrastructure,**
Kellogg Brown and Root

Communication mechanisms add significantly to the success of a virtual team. Whether it is weekly telephone conferences, net meetings, or an e-mail system with structure, having formalized communication systems is a critical success factor. Virtual team members must make individual decisions about what to do with information they receive. Without some way to check for understanding, misunderstandings can easily occur. Some communication considerations include:

➤ Communicate frequently to maintain task focus and to nurture relationships.

➤ Note the perceived urgency and importance of a piece of information.

➤ Describe your context vividly so that teammates have a mental picture of your situation.

➤ Establish and honor communication guidelines.

➤ Let other teammates get to know a little about you personally.

➤ Ask questions when unsure of something (e.g., due to language barriers or technical difficulties).

➤ Do a superior job of writing what you mean and meaning what you write.

➤ Share your reactions to and thoughts about e-mails and messages from your teammate—let them know what you are thinking.

Virtual workers are certainly not a new phenomenon. Salespeople have historically worked out of their homes or their vehicles to service customer territories. Many were part of a sales team, organized by region or product lines. This worked because the following criteria were in place:

➤ They were committed to a common organizational purpose.

➤ They could only achieve their personal goals by working together to meet organizational goals.

➤ They had independent tasks yet needed each other to accomplish their work.

➤ They were accountable to the same leader.

These salespeople pioneered the "virtual" working framework. They rarely came into the company office because their work was done elsewhere. And they did this without the benefits of today's technology.

"THE BIGGEST ISSUES ARE DISCIPLINE to meet agreed-to time frames, an incredibly high need for effective communication and the lack of relationships with people who primarily interact via nonpersonal methods."

— **Shelley McLean, Principle, CONVERGE Group, Calgary, Canada**

More and more professions face these same work requirements. The work is where the customer is, and that is often far from the "home" office. This has generated the need to effectively structure people and work without the advantage of regular face-to-face contact. "Working virtually" means working with people you cannot see. Some face-to-face contact is necessary to build trust, address tough issues, and ensure alignment with company direction, but the work itself may be geographically dispersed. When an organization needs employees to work remotely to sell, provide services, or produce products yet wants the benefits of teamwork, the only alternative is to form virtual teams. This is a good choice when a collaborative culture best meets the needs of the customer, the organization, and the team members.

An additional factor generating the demand for virtual work opportunities is the workers themselves. For a variety of reasons, people are opting for the flexibility of working from home offices or satellite offices. Whether driven by customer requirements, employee desires, or business economics, unique issues face teams working virtually.

STAYING CONNECTED

Staying connected to other members of the team is another critical issue facing virtual teams. Consider the experience of Les Komanecky, a manager for General Motors in the U.S. Les requested to work in a virtual location to avoid a cross country move. He had two children in high school and did not want to move them. In addition, Les was ready for a new job challenge and wanted to try his hand at consulting. The virtual assignment gave him the opportunity to pursue a consulting career while staying with General Motors.

"MY VIRTUAL EXPERIENCE WAS GOOD. I enjoyed the freedom, the comfort of working from home, and the trust showed me. I found myself more productive in the virtual office. Getting coffee took me only a few minutes to walk downstairs and fill up my cup. In the traditional office environment, the act of getting coffee includes human interaction. It can take thirty minutes to get that coffee."

— Les Komanecky, Manager, General Motors

Systems and structures must be in place to have a virtual team experience work for the remote members. Some examples include:

➤ The main office must be supportive and responsive, providing information, supplies, or help of any kind.

➤ Good communications infrastructure and advanced technology are a must, including good computers and peripherals. Most of the communications with other team members and customers is via e-mail.

➤ With more information and work activities utilizing the Web, it is imperative that virtual offices have high-speed communications and a computer system that can utilize those resources.

➤ Team members in a virtual office must take it upon themselves to call other people in order to stay connected. The team members in the central office must not forget about those in virtual offices.

➤ The organization must create situations that bring all team members together on a regular basis. This re-energizes those in the virtual office and builds a better bond within the entire team.

USE H.E.A.R.T.

Work teams made up of people in different locations must have processes and procedures that enable them to function independently but also as a team. The goal of virtual teams is to accommodate the diverse geographical requirements while still giving the organization the team benefits of synergy, creativity, and flexibility. The five critical team processes described in chapter 2 must be in place to get optimal virtual teamwork. The following sections describe how these team processes apply to virtual teams.

Honest Dialogue

The organization must invest in adequate communication mechanisms. Being able to communicate with one another is a priority for virtual teams. Based on the team's responsibilities, each member must discuss the key topics facing the team. This sets the stage for future interaction. Key topics for virtual teams include agreeing on how to complete their interdependent tasks and how to ask for help. Bringing up and discussing performance issues is never easy, and in a virtual environment, if a foundation is not in place, these constructive discussions may never occur.

Building adequate levels of trust within the team is critical. This has to be considered in every aspect of the team's work. It can be initiated during the formation of the team but must continue in all communications and dialogue. Often, it is unresolved issues that cause team members to doubt each other.

Effective Problem Solving and Decision Making
Working interdependently, using agreed-to decision-making processes, and being disciplined to follow through are challenges for many virtual teams. Some decisions are made by the managers and communicated to the team members. Other decisions fall to the team or rest with the individual team members. For a virtual team, clear, agreed-to decision-making processes are needed for each scenario. Decisions can help solve problems, but without clear processes, decisions also can generate additional problems. An effective decision-making process is intended to keep the team on task by involving the right people.

Accountability
Virtual teams need a shared purpose to justify their existence as a team. They must have the ability to track their work, hold discussions, and resolve problems. Having regular performance information is essential to the virtual team member. The information must be timely, useful, and specific. To build team spirit, teams must also be held accountable for overall progress and performance as a unit. By clearly defining the team's tasks and responsibilities, the team can set goals in support of its overall purpose. Along with accolades, performance or other team issues must be addressed in a timely and appropriate manner. Every virtual leader must develop the skills required to coach within a virtual team framework.

Virtual teams are different from on-site teams, and their norms must build a strong foundation that grows with every interaction. Virtual team norms reflect the dynamics that come from working physically separate from their teammates. The following sections offer some examples of norms that should be followed by a virtual team.

Listening
➤ Allow equal air time on the telephone or Internet.

➤ Make sure everyone gets a chance to speak.

Information Sharing

➤ Always consider what you are going to say and how you are going to say it—before you say it!

➤ Reread your e-mails for possible misinterpretations before sending them.

➤ Consider carefully who should get a copy of your messages.

➤ Choose an appropriate tone of voice when leaving telephone messages.

➤ Keep communication simple and clear.

➤ Check to see if you got the right message across.

➤ Make sure every message goes to everyone (unless totally personal in nature).

➤ Agree on the kind of information to be communicated, to whom, and by what media.

➤ Keep most e-talk about business.

➤ Keep each other posted on personal events and share funny stories.

➤ Show discretion by knowing what is appropriate to discuss, when, and how.

Decision Making

➤ Check the level of agreement to a decision by asking for a comment from each team member.

Conflict Resolution

➤ Do not use any "electronic" form of communication to resolve conflict regarding personal issues.

➤ Address the conflict in a timely manner.

➤ Address the conflict privately with the people involved.

Responsibilities

➤ Clarify who is responsible for what at the end of each meeting or conversation.

➤ Follow up oral conversations with written documentation.

➤ Check e-mail and voice mail daily.

➤ Respond to information requests in a timely manner.

➤ Follow through on commitments.

Meetings

➤ Establish meeting protocol.

➤ Always know who is in the meeting.

➤ Have the speaking person identify himself or herself until voices are easily recognized.

➤ Hold regular project review meetings—face-to-face—to maintain interpersonal relationships.

➤ Focus task business electronically and convene the team face-to-face to handle tough issues.

➤ Consider time zone issues and share time zone inconvenience.

Training

➤ Develop skills for using the technology appropriately.

➤ Deploy good time management practices.

➤ Learn e-mail and voice mail protocol (see figure 6-1 for some guidelines).

Respectful Relationships and Trust

The building blocks for the virtual team are trust, respect, empathy, and regular contact. Virtual teams are formed one relationship at a time just like in any other type of team. A key difference is that the majority of relationship building occurs from a distance.

When it comes to doing most of your interaction from a distance, building trust can be a challenge. This trust has to be earned. It is not built overnight and usually results after repeated experiences yield positive results. In a recent study of virtual teamwork involving people from all over the world, trust building was identified as one factor that separated high performance from poor to average performance. "Swift trust" is the willingness of team members to proactively take initiative and follow through with their commitments[1].

The key is to allow for adequate contact, so competence and trustworthiness can be demonstrated and a solid relationship can be formed. The group members and dynamics, the tasks to be performed, and the required level of interdependence determine the importance and type of relationships. Although people do not need to have lunch together every day to have a trusting and respectful relationship, most do need to have a solid personal connection to feel some sense of belonging to a team. Trust comes from having knowledge and experience. Team members must understand each other and be confident in each other's competence. Then, everyone must be committed to the same goals while accommodating as much as possible each individual team member's need for contact and inclusion.

For example, consider the advice of Carol Talbot, an independent consultant and trainer working in Dubai, United Arab Emirates. After years of working solo as an independent consultant, Carol joined a small virtual team of about nine people. These team members work from their separate homes but build a team spirit by meeting once a month and having a social get-together once a month. At each team meeting, one member of the team is asked to briefly present his or her background and competencies so that the other team members can increase their knowledge and understanding of the competencies and knowledge held within

---

1. Hardt and Brynteson, "Swift Virtual Trust," 1998.

the entire team. With this information, opportunity for collaboration is recognized.

"ALTHOUGH WE ARE ALL DIFFERENT—with backgrounds in HR, psychology, customer service, etc.—there is respect for each member's attributes, common values, and an openness to share and learn from each other. Common values seem to be a pivotal key—and trust! We keep in contact as a group by e-mail and contribute to a monthly newsletter to keep us in touch with achievements. Soon we will have an intranet bulletin board up and running."

— Carol Talbot, Consultant

Building trusting relationships is a number one priority for virtual teams. Steps that help include:

➤ Spending time formally and informally to get to know each other

➤ Raising issues immediately

➤ Addressing people directly and appropriately

➤ Resolving differences to maintain high levels of trust

Although there are other important aspects to a team's process, the critical aspects are honest dialogue, effective decision-making processes, accountability, relationships, and trust—all of these must be in place to meet the needs of virtual teams. Paying attention to the dynamics of the team and having adequate levels of structure to know when things are working or not working can help keep the team on track. The team processes must be customized to recognize the unique challenges facing any team that functions virtually.

Figure 6-1: Suggested E-mail and Voice Mail Protocol

- Answer messages promptly.
- Send simple, straightforward messages.
- Send group mail when all recipients need it.
- Remove people from your distribution lists.
- Ask to be removed from distribution lists.
- Use subject lines in e-mails and be specific in describing your topic.
- Use attachments sparingly.
- Use Web sites for communicating large documents.
- Be specific in all your communications.
- Update your outgoing message to inform callers when you are out of the office.
- Forward messages with care and consideration.

BUILDING AN INFRASTRUCTURE

We have discussed the importance of communication mechanisms, technology resources, and relationship building. These elements must be integrated and connected into a process that routinely monitors and supports virtual teams. In fact, when people are interviewed about their experiences in virtual teams, they are quick to point out that it is 90 percent people and 10 percent technology[2].

Consider the experience of Ann Price-Perkins, a former consultant with General Motors in the United States. Ann served as a member of two virtual organizations. In one, the organization was structured from the beginning because members lived in various parts of the country. There was never any consideration given to moving everyone to where the office was. She describes her first virtual team experience as poor. It was particularly difficult because it was not only virtual, but self-managing—a double challenge. The organization did not sponsor team building, and

2. Lipnack and Stamps, *Virtual Teams*, 1997.

training and development needs of the team members were unclear. In-person meetings were held quarterly with agendas full of strategy, structure, and action planning, with little time given to team building.

"AS A VIRTUAL ORGANIZATION, HIDDEN AGENDAS were easier to hide, and trust was difficult, with lots of fear of unseen power plays and a sense of isolation from 'the action'. Training and development needs were not as easily perceived or identified as more frequent interaction would encourage, and the fear factor did not make it easy for individuals to voice developmental needs."

— Ann Price-Perkins, Consultant

Ann had another opportunity to try virtual teamwork, and this time, her experience was better. Time was spent up-front defining the team's task. The team dynamics didn't overshadow the team's ability to work together and get its tasks done. One of the strongest factors contributing to virtual team success is a clear focus on the work to be done[3].

"THERE WAS A TON OF EFFORT GIVEN TO COMMUNICATION of vision, strategies, and structure—both as information flowed and in the exchange of ideas/perceptions."

— Ann Price-Perkins, Consultant

In addition to what we know makes any organization work— a shared vision, clear direction, defined roles and responsibilities, and adequate training—for virtual teams, adding the following infrastructure could help address many of the special challenges presented by people working separately from each other:

➤ A strong mentoring and/or partnering system

---

3. Hardt and Brynteson, "Swift Virtual Trust," 1998.

➤ Task-orientation and proactive work

➤ A clear and specific mission for the work to be done

➤ Shared leadership and responsibility for the work and the team's effectiveness;

➤ Commitment to very extensive communication

➤ Focus on personal development to strengthen interdependence

Because location and daily contact are missing, what can serve as a connector of individuals in a virtual, yet highly functional team? Three key factors are *relationships, technology, and leadership*. The goal is to maintain team spirit over a physical distance while asking people to work separately. To utilize today's available technology, the company must provide the right resources. And overall, managing the team and leading it to reach the desired goals and objectives will not happen without effective leadership. Because the team leader is not physically close enough to lend a hand, having the structure and relationships in place to help is important. The following sections list some ideas for addressing these key issues with virtual teams.

ISSUE #1

Lack of Relationships between People Who See Each Other Infrequently

Things To Do to Prevent or Resolve This Problem:

1. Bring team members together when first forming the team so they can form relationships.

2. Host annual state-of-the-business meetings with everyone in attendance to communicate progress and future direction.

3. Build time for relationship building into every meeting agenda.

4. Link virtual team members with on-site members as mentors or "buddies" to keep information flowing throughout the team.

5. Organize periodic face-to-face contact with members of the team, though this does not have to include every team member every time.

6. Celebrate successes and progress in fun ways.

7. Organize problem-solving sessions to address challenges.

8. Target discussions and activities that raise the issue of trust so team members can clearly identify what trust means to them.

ISSUE #2

Adequate Technology and Skills to Successfully Work From a Virtual Location

Things To Do to Prevent or Resolve This Problem:

1. Use technology to build, exchange, and manipulate data and information.

2. Avoid using technology to resolve people issues.

3. Build a solid communications infrastructure.

4. Provide and maintain appropriate levels of technology. With more information and work activities utilizing the Web, it is imperative that virtual offices have high-speed communications and a computer system that can utilize those resources.

5. Select a communications and project management system and make it work.

6. Train virtual team members to fully use the technology.

ISSUE #3

Effective Leadership and Management from a Distance

Things To Do to Prevent or Resolve this Problem:

1. Clearly define the team leader and manager roles with a focus on motivating, coaching, training, and advising.

2. Teach and coach self-control and personal accountability.

3. Strive for autonomy balanced with clear direction.

4. Establish and implement a performance management system with defined performance metrics.

5. Coordinate activities in a manner that involves all players; if some team members work in the same location as the team manager or leader, include remote team members as well as on-site team members in discussions and projects.

6. Pay attention to team member performance; praise achievers and address performance problems quickly.

7. Be clear with team members about where they should go for help and resources.

8. Address inappropriate behaviors immediately.

MEASURING SUCCESS

Traditional metrics can report the output of any organization. When it comes to virtual teams, beyond the numbers, what can we watch for? When measuring the success of a team, look at three performance areas:[4]

> ➤ Measurement of performance based on the team's actual output—i.e., is it on-time? Is it on budget? Have quality standards been met?

---

4. Hackman, *Groups That Work*, 1990.

➤ Measurement of satisfaction—i.e., did members enjoy being a part of the team? Were they challenged? Were they rewarded? Would they want to repeat the experience?

➤ Measurement of the team's processes—i.e., did team members benefit from their participation on the team? Did the team learn to improve its efficiency or effectiveness?

Reading the stories of the virtual team members embedded in this chapter, it is notable that they mention their *satisfaction* and their team *processes* but rarely their *contribution to the output* of the team. This suggests that organizations should remember the key metrics of contribution and performance as an area for focus and improvement.

SELECTING THE RIGHT PEOPLE FOR VIRTUAL TEAMS

Team selection is another critical issue, especially for virtual teams. Two primary success factors for virtual team members are self-motivation and the ability to thrive in a nonstandard work environment. For example, consider the experience of Denny Teasdle, a team leader and trainer working for Saturn in the U.S. Denny worked as both a team member and a team leader in a virtual team setting. He was on a virtual team because he did not live near the main hub of business and the majority of his work necessitated travel so there was no business reason to relocate.

"THE TEAM MEMBERS WHO STRUGGLED THE MOST were the ones who needed strong direction and supervision. Because it is extremely easy to gain a 'stepchild' mentality, it is critical for the virtual team members to have a clear understanding of their roles and how they support the total business venture. All team members need a sense of value in their work, but I believe it is even more critical in a virtual environment. Receiving regular feedback on how the virtual players are doing as individuals and how they are impacting the total business performance is also critical. This is important in both formal and informal communications, as well as in goal setting and performance measurement. Virtual team members need proof that they are an essential part of the team."

— Denny Teasdle, Retired Saturn Consultant and Team Leader

Organizations must pay attention to the internal virtual team dynamics and the support systems within the organization that enable people to do their work. It takes both to create successful virtual teams. Leaders and managers must ask questions, resolve problems, and create a disciplined work framework to support the natural chaos that comes with virtual teams. The success of virtual teams starts with finding the right team members. Building infrastructure and ongoing support mechanisms allows these individuals to make their virtual location a nonissue when it comes to getting work done.

Understanding the characteristics and important skills of each virtual team member can enable organizations to set up virtual teams for success. In general, the key skills to look for in virtual team members are shown in figure 6-2.

Figure 6-2: Key Virtual Team Member Skills

Communication skills

- Uses right words.
- Manages nonverbal communication.
- Thinks before responding.

Honesty

- Tells the truth.
- Meets obligations.
- Behaves in a trustworthy manner.

Tact

- Considers others' feelings and situation.
- Deals in a nonoffensive manner.
- Understands when and how to raise sensitive or emotional issues.

Questioning skills

- Asks great questions.
- Paraphrases answers.

Time management

- Respects time frames.
- Meets commitments.

Team management

- Understands team dynamics.
- Constructively deals with tasks and issues.
- Easily builds relationships.
- Maintains relationships.
- Addresses conflict constructively.

Consider also the experience of Toby Andreassen, who is a senior partner and trainer for TripleWin Nordic AB, a training and consulting company in Scandinavia. Toby is a member of the

TripleWin global leadership team that maintains a global network of consultants and trainers in the areas of teamwork, leadership, and customer service. Building any team is a challenge but adding in the elements of a variety of countries and virtual locations increases the challenge.

"YOU NEED PEOPLE WHO FIND THE CONTENT OF THE PROJECT OR PRODUCT interesting and rewarding to work with. More than one person in the team must drive the team forward. A lot of communication is needed (personally I need to hear the teammates' voices now and then or see them). There must be continuous improvement including content and best practice discussions, and a common understanding and respect for teamwork."

— **Toby Andreassen, Senior Partner and Trainer,
TripleWin Nordic AB**

One method for discerning whether or not the team members have these skills is to use an assessment. Assessments help us understand the attributes of people who typically succeed in virtual team roles. The Virtual Team Attributes Assessment shown in figure 6-3 can help determine a person's suitability for virtual teamwork.

CONCLUSION

Virtual teams offer many benefits. There are many unique aspects of this type of team to manage. As one virtual team member explained:

"YOU DO NOT WORK UNDER A MICROSCOPE. You are trusted by virtue of working separately from your manager. I love the flexibility regarding work hours, and our customers like it because we are closer to our actual market. However, there are some downsides. I feel out of the loop on just about everything. The people at the home office are more informed and involved in idea sharing. I feel my job is less secure because any cuts would be made from the virtual team quicker than the home office team. The other big problem is our virtual office gives 'slackers' too much ability to hide. There are people that abuse the freedom our location provides. They come to work late, and work fewer hours than expected; they cheat the company. This behavior goes undetected, and it is not fair to the company or to me."

Leaders must lead and managers must manage their teams, whether they are seen daily or managed from a distance. The top leader becomes the glue to hold together scattered parts of the virtual team.

Figure 6-3: Virtual Team Attributes Self-Assessment

Instructions: *Check the boxes of the attributes you consistently demonstrate.*

❏ I enjoy communicating through e-mail.

❏ I am a self-starter.

❏ I like to work on projects independently.

❏ I enjoy talking on the telephone.

❏ I enjoy writing down my ideas, plans, and projects.

❏ I prefer having my own projects.

❏ I solve problems effectively on my own without input, information, and clarification from others.

❏ I enjoy learning new things on the computer.

❏ I am well organized.

❏ I like to plan my own work.

❏ It is easy for me to ask for help and input.

❏ I thrive on solving problems that arise unexpectedly.

❏ I am comfortable defining and clarifying my roles and responsibilities.

❏ I take the time to inform others about critical information about my activities.

❏ I enjoy building on the ideas of others.

❏ I am good at clarifying others' statements to understand their points of view.

❏ I like having well-established procedures and policies.

❏ I like structuring my own work schedule.

❏ I am able to solve computer problems myself.

❏ I prefer working with minimal direction.

❏ I like contributing to a team's efforts.

❏ I value feedback and ideas from others.

Total of checked boxes _____

Figure 6-3: Virtual Team Attributes Self-Assessment

Scoring

0-7   Only a few attributes were selected that are found in successful virtual team members; therefore, there is a low probability of success as a virtual team member.

8-15   Some attributes were selected that are found in successful virtual team members; this team member may require additional training or support to succeed as part of a virtual team.

16-22 Many attributes were selected that are found in successful virtual team members; therefore, there is a high probability of success as a virtual team member.

CHAPTER 7

Quick-Change Teams

> **DEFINITION:** *A small group of people trained in team skills and responsible for turning out products or services without the advantage of stable team membership. The group has frequent member changes yet must work daily on interdependent tasks.*

WORK TEAMS IN RAPIDLY CHANGING ORGANIZATIONS rarely stay together for long periods of time. The investment in team development is wasted, or at least compromised, if it requires teams to stay intact. Most team-development and team-building initiatives strive to build a unit of people into a high-performance team. This investment assumes the team will stay together for the long term or at least until the task is accomplished. The reality is that most organizations experience perpetual change, and with these changes, teams are frequently disbanded and reformed.

Many teams are set up to be temporary. They are design teams or problem-solving teams with a specific focus. Quick-change teams are different because they are intended to act like intact, natural teams, with one difference: frequent membership changes. The goal is to have the team quickly get down to business, focus on the task, keep distractions to a minimum, and remain open to membership changes. The changes are based on employee retirements, transfers, self-initiated job changes, major reorganization, team performance issues, or continuous improvement initiatives. The goal is to create a framework for a work environment that allows for teamwork in the face of constant change. In this vein, we are using teams to create a collaborative environment in which people team up to achieve a worthwhile and important goal. A collaborative environment refers to the extent team members communicate openly, share problems and information, help coordinate work, and focus on getting the task completed. Members in this collaborative environment have common skills and approaches that allow them to work together efficiently and effectively across a variety of settings and with different people[1].

Rarely can organizations find sufficient time to rebuild teams after every change. Organizations in a high state of flux would rather focus on building flexibility into teams so that when members change, they can quickly regroup and become functional. Stability is usually a positive factor for teams. However, the reality for most organizations is not stability. Although the basic principles of teamwork and team development are still valid, the aspect of constant change must be factored in. Revised approaches, new models, and acceptance of change as an environmental reality allow quick-change teams to find their footing.

Teams are not obsolete. They can still contribute in this new high-change environment in spite of the obstacles involved. We need to change our paradigm of how we organize, train, and facilitate teams. The key is to focus on creating a collaborative environment that capitalizes on the abilities of the team members, no matter which team they are working on. A key success factor for quick-change teams is the structure of the team itself. If the purpose is clear and the structure is right, quick-change teams are set up to perform.

---

1. Beyerlein, Freedman, McGee, and Moran, *Beyond Teams*, 2002.

The notion of quick-change teams is new to team discussions. It requires a paradigm shift away from intact *team* investment to team *member* investment. Most people enjoy being a member of a high-performance team. They feel pride, satisfaction, joy in their work, and affection for their teammates. That experience is lasting. When the team is dismantled, those team members can still carry with them the knowledge and experience they gained during their team experience. Any company that moves team members around may find that positive cross-pollination takes place when members of one team are combined with different team members.

The paradigm shift is not only in the approach used in team building but also in what the organization realizes and expects out of the investment it makes in teams. This means a fundamental change in expectations, as well as a change in the methodology used to structure teams. The goal when working with quick-change teams is to accelerate team development and to build a foundation that supports teamwork. This is achieved by training team members to function effectively in a team environment and providing effective team management. With skills and leadership in place, an organization can accommodate frequent team membership changes.

THE AIRLINE INDUSTRY'S CREW RESOURCE MANAGEMENT PROCESS

A wonderful model of quick-change teams is found in the aviation industry. The task of getting an aircraft from one place to another remains essentially the same, but the crew is different every time. The airlines have created a team structure with all of the basic team elements in place to accommodate the constantly changing membership of the team. In this context, team management is called Crew Resource Management (CRM).

Up until the 1970s, the shipboard model of the captain being totally in charge of everything (command and control) was standard in aviation. In that decade, investigation of several dreadful accidents revealed the fact that pilot fault was strongly implicated in 70 percent of accidents. Officials realized that the existing model of flight management was failing. CRM is the aviation industry's attempt to deal with this situation. Every flight crew member, under internationally agreed-to regulations, undergoes CRM training on a regular basis. Each is scored on his or her CRM skill as well as his or her technical skill. Cabin crews are also being included in CRM training, and the model is also beginning to be introduced into engineering and other sectors of aviation companies.

The CRM philosophy is that every member of a given flight crew must know how to work efficiently and effectively with every other member even if they have never met before. For each flight there is a preflight briefing during which goals are set and norms of working are reached (i.e., who flies what leg, who will do what in the case of emergency, how time will be managed, who is responsible for what area, etc.). Naturally, the emotional bonds that exist in long-term teams do not form. However the approach does ensure that the down side implicit in working with strangers (e.g., lack of understanding, poor communication, fear of other's authority) is reduced considerably. The CRM process replaces a typical team's responsibilty (and often struggle) to organize itself and to decide who has what authority. It provides a structure that gives the crew a quick start in becoming a functional team. Time and energy is saved at the beginning of every flight. Since the ability to work together efficiently and effectively as a team is vital, especially when an aircraft is in a difficult or dangerous situation, this process is highly supported and accepted by the aviation industry.

The introduction of CRM is believed to be a huge factor behind increasing aviation safety. The same approach is now being introduced into many similar areas, such as surgery, firefighting, oil rig work, and others. Naturally, the approach could not be copied exactly into any given situation, but some of the ideas behind CRM may be useful in a wide range of industries.

OPTIMIZING PRODUCTIVITY OF QUICK-CHANGE TEAMS: TIME IS OF THE ESSENCE

For a team concept to work optimally in high-change organizations, a group of people must come together quickly, work on a task, and not lose any time when it moves on to a new team or a different task—with little or no decline in performance. Without building this ability into their teams, organizations experiencing significant and constant change might find team structures unworkable. However, with the right goals, individuals can develop a quick-change mentality.

I recently worked as a member of a seven person consulting team in South Korea. We had never worked as a team before; in fact, we originated from the U.S., Belgium, and South Korea. The first time we were together was the day before our work began. This quick-change team was successful because we clearly contracted our roles, divided the work appropriately, maintained open lines of communication, and trusted each others' competence. We had no time for formal team and trust building. We had to assume the best about each other and do our own best work. The project, and this team, was successful because the right players were on the team and the mission was clear. And we were all committed to success and would not accept less.

A quick-change mentality means having the following elements in place:

➤ Changes in team membership are expected and welcomed.

➤ Team members bring integrity, dependability, and reliability into the team relationship.

➤ Team members are competent—every team member brings skills and assets to the team.

➤ Individual roles and responsibilities are clear yet connected to overall team and organization performance.

➤ There is a strong focus on the task assigned to the team.

➤ Clear team norms are in place and agreed to.

➤ There is the right balance of independence and interdependence for task accomplishment.

➤ The situation is approached with a positive attitude and commitment to success.

➤ Basic team skills are developed and used to sustain team performance.

➤ Leaders split their time between sustaining a level of team performance and emphasizing individual performance.

The next sections of this chapter explore a variety of scenarios to highlight the key aspects of these quick-change team elements.

SCENARIO 1

How to Handle Changes in Team Membership

Upon being hired at a car assembly plant, John was assigned to the Door Assembly Team. He quickly learned the team's tasks and got comfortable with his teammates. Six months later, the organization announced it was downsizing its operations and eliminating one shift of operations. The result was that every team was rearranged. Some team members remained together, but every team gained new players. The company no longer employed some of John's teammates. The company needed the remaining team members to regroup into their new teams and to quickly reach a high level of performance. Instead, the teams became dysfunctional. Quality suffered and production goals were missed. Conflict between people was obvious. Instead of the expected two-week adjustment period, performance issues continued for six months.

Question: Why were these team members unable to get back on track quickly?

Key Lessons
Expectations are set when you hire new people into an organization. How the job is described sets the stage. If a person (like John) is told he will be a member of one team for the long term, he will embrace that idea, work at building strong relationships, and get comfortable. If, at a later date, his team is forced to change, he will probably resist that change. He might feel anger and frustration and be unwilling to accept his new team assignment. He will be distracted from doing his job by the relationship issues that have surfaced.

Changing the paradigm for teams is a first step. It begins with explaining to people that they will be asked to work with a variety of people, on a variety of teams, and in a number of areas based on the needs of the business. This may eliminate some of the resistance to changing team assignments and decrease incidents of nonperformance. People still might miss their old teammates, but the change will not be a total surprise to them or outside the scope of their employment agreement.

SCENARIO 2

The Importance of Developing Individual Roles and Responsibilities

When Ana started working for a new insurance company, her responsibilities were outlined to her in terms of team responsibilities. The manager explained that she would be expected to learn all of the team tasks. Experienced team members would train her until she was proficient in all tasks. However, several team members retired at the beginning of the year and were replaced by new hires. The team's performance began to slide, and the team leader was unable to determine the cause or quickly address the growing performance issues.

Question: What triggered the performance decline and complicated the diagnosis and problem solving?

Key Lessons

Intact teams develop high levels of interdependence. In fact, interdependence is encouraged. But when teams change, it can be a hindrance. Within a team, members assume various roles and also develop a range of expertise. If individual performance is not monitored, performance issues can be masked by the overall group performance. Then, if the more skilled team members leave, the skill of the team can fall quickly and unexpectedly. The void results in nonperformance.

Team performance tracking must be balanced with individual performance assessment. When a task needs to be performed, on any given day, every person needs to know it is his or her job to perform that task. Overdependence on a few team members can hurt a team's performance when natural or accelerated attrition occurs. In today's quick-change world, *every* team member must be competent.

In quick-change teams, the leader's role is central to the team structure. The team leader is responsible for training new team members, managing any voids created when a key player moves, and making sure team issues are quickly addressed. It is possible, but not always common, that an experienced group of people can come together and quickly establish an effective working environment. In most cases, the leader will need to help it happen. A hands-off leadership approach is dangerous in teams with frequent membership changes. Establishing the right hierarchy helps quick-change teams achieve success.

SCENARIO 3

Ensuring Basic Critical Skills for Quick-change Teams

Annually, a national bank gives each of its teams two days of team-building training. During those days, the team participates in get-to-know-you activities, problem-solving tasks, and team initiatives. A team-building consultant facilitates the event. After the simulated team events, the group discusses what they did well, what they could do better, and how this learning can be transferred to their real team tasks. For the most part, it is a fun two days and the group is energized. One or two of the team members think it is a waste of time and just want to go and do real work, but the majority of the participants feel the event builds stronger relationships and team spirit.

During the year, in between these off-site team-building exercises, the group experiences changes in team members and a major change in the bank operations. The team leader is at a loss for how to address the resulting problems because the team had already completed its team building.

Question: What skills were missing?

Key Lessons

For any team, some amount of team building is important. For quick-change teams, the content of the team building must focus on skills that transfer easily when team members change. When each individual member has team skills, the team has the building blocks of effective teamwork. In addition, teams cannot be built around an annual event. Teams need some level of development with every member change or with significant task changes.

Figure 7-1 shows some essential skills for working in a quick-change team. Team-building events and training of these interpersonal skills is a wise investment for organizations using team structures.

Figure 7-1: Required Quick-Change Team Skills

Meeting Participation
Working within a meeting agenda; facilitating and participating in productive discussions

Personal Competence
Skills and assets that will help accomplish the task, integrity, and dependability

Problem Solving
Following a basic problem-solving approach to reach an acceptable solution

Listening
Engaging in active listening by building on others' points; paraphrasing ideas

Assertiveness
Expressing ideas with confidence; convincing others to listen and accept ideas

Conflict Resolution
Working through conflict situations; listening and actively talking through disagreements; finding solutions

Decision Making
Reaching decisions as part of a team

Quick-Change Team Skills Assessment

With quick-change teams emerging as a new type of team, time should be spent determining the skills that will help team members be successful. When asked what accounts for the success of a team, the consistent answer is "it is imperative to select the right people."[2] Figure 7-2 offers an assessment that can be used to identify quick-change team skills. Each prospective team member should use this assessment to determine his or her level of readiness to be a member of a quick-change team. Once identified, selection or development decisions can target the key areas.

---

2. Larson and LaDasto, *Teamwork*, 1989.

Figure 7-2: Quick-Change Team Assessment

Directions: *Use the following checklist to determine your level of readiness to be a member of a quick-change team. Put a checkmark next to the items you feel you have mastered. Consider developing the items not mastered to future assist you in becoming a skilled quick-change team member.*

❏ I enjoy new experiences and people.

❏ I meet new people easily.

❏ I build trusting relationships easily.

❏ I request feedback on my behavior and performance.

❏ I follow meeting agenda and processes.

❏ I state problems clearly.

❏ I sell my ideas and alternatives.

❏ I admit mistakes.

❏ I assist others in identifying next steps.

❏ I listen attentively to others.

❏ I encourage others to share their ideas.

❏ I deal effectively with my anger and frustration.

❏ I explain information clearly and accurately.

❏ I clarify issues effectively.

❏ I ask questions frequently.

❏ I encourage new ideas, suggestions, and methods.

❏ I resolve misunderstandings.

❏ I implement decisions.

❏ I help others when they need it.

❏ I ask for help when I need it.

❏ I remain open to new people and their opinions.

❏ I work independently.

❏ I work interdependently.

❏ I accept direction from others.

❏ I follow through on my commitments.

❏ I tackle challenges with a positive attitude and approach.

SCENARIO 4

The Leader's Role in Quick-change Teams

Peter has been a sales manager in car dealerships for twelve years. He is effective in getting his team members to understand what has to be done. He prefers to manage by getting the group to work effectively and then stepping back and letting them manage themselves. This worked well for Peter before his teams began to transition new members in and out on a regular basis. Peter struggled with having to repeatedly provide direction and guidance to the team. His other managerial tasks suffered. After several months of poor team performance, Peter went to his supervisor and asked to be reassigned.

> **Question: What leadership style increases a leader's success with quick-change teams?**

Key Lessons

Leading mature, intact teams requires a different leadership approach than leading quick-change teams. Leaders must be skilled in working with teams and in knowing how to provide the right amount of direction and how to help the team no matter how new or unstable the membership is. With a maturing team, the leader can be less directly involved as team members pick up responsibility for managing themselves. Most quick-change teams do not have the chance to reach advanced stages of maturity. Managers must stay actively involved, working with both the individuals and the team as a whole.

The best quick-change team leadership approach combines a directive, teaching style that includes focusing on both clear team and individual responsibilities. There is no time for ambiguity in quick-change teams. Quick-change team members want to know what to do, whom to work with, when the task is due, and where resources are located—in other words, what is expected of each team member individually and as part of the team. In addition, quick-change team members want to know who their resources are, including the team leader. At the same time, when someone has mastered the task and the team is functioning effectively, the leadership style can and should become less directive.[3]

THINGS TO DO TO DEVELOP SUCCESSFUL QUICK-CHANGE TEAMS

A key to having mature quick-change teams is to have mature quick-change team members. When team members accept change as a given, the time that had been spent resisting the change can be spent getting reestablished. With any team effort, the higher the level of trust and respect between team members, the better the relationships can be. However, the time necessary to build a high level of rapport may not be available. Be realistic in expectations for any team that is kept unstable by membership change; build the best team possible given these circumstances.

By their very nature, quick-change teams do not have time on their side. To offset this, the following actions can be taken:

1. Early in the process, use team-development activities to assimilate new team members. Focus on essential information: some pertinent background information, team norms, roles and responsibilities, and team goals. Have the team develop the process to include what it needs every team member to know.

2. Help the team members maintain strong working relationships by appointing managers who can address problems quickly with minimal disruption to team performance. The clearer the roles and responsibilities and the stronger the manager is in problem solving, decision making, and conflict resolution, the better team problems can be addressed.

---

3. Hersey, *Situational Leadership*, 1984.

3. Structure the jobs and tasks with standardized work practices. If all team members are trained to perform the tasks in the same ways, changing team members is less disruptive.

4. Define each member's relationship to the team in terms of the role to be filled and the results to be produced. Each member must understand what he or she will be held accountable for and measured against in terms of performance.

5. Build adequate trust among the team members through communication and fair standards of performance. Address nonperformance issues in a timely and consistent fashion.

6. Train people to work effectively in teams. From the beginning, let everyone know he or she is required to work in a team approach, with regular changes in teammates and even job tasks. That's the job. Then, make sure everyone has a basic level of team skills to make this doable.

7. Ensure there is adequate help available to the team. This includes the leader. Having subject matter experts to help with problem solving keeps the team doing what it is supposed to do, which is to produce products or services.

8. Formalize an exit process for those leaving the team, and allow this ending to be the beginning of a new team.

9. Involve the teams in developing their own strategies to cope with the changes. Determine what would most help the individuals/teams accept change.

10. Explain the business reasons behind the changes. Involve the teams in finding ways they can improve. Provide information and increase the understanding for the need to change.

11. Make sure that policies, practices, and systems accept the quick-change team structure, including time for team assimilation, training, and team leader support.

CONCLUSION

"AS THE COMPETITIVE LANDSCAPE SHIFTS, those who are quickest to adopt the advanced social technology of collaborative design are likely to be the winners. Collaborative organizations enable the optimum development of the intellectual and social capital that increases the financial capital of the company."

— from *Beyond Teams: Building the Collaborative Organization*

There is certainly a trade-off when an organization has quick-change teams instead of stable natural work teams. With quick-change teams, the interdependence is compromised to allow for membership change. Training, facilitating, and norm sessions are helpful but not sufficient in creating strong team bonding, cohesion, and effectiveness, all of which take time and experience. It is usually the interdependence that leads to synergy in teams. This means the sum is greater than the parts because people build on each other's strengths, and the results can often exceed what is typically achieved.

What benefits are gained by using quick-change versus individual workers? This goes back to the research on teams itself. There is a social need that is often met when individuals affiliate with a team. There is also flexibility gained in having individuals accountable for their team's performance. It is not just "What is my job?" but also "What is our team required to do?" Any type of successful team can contribute performance gains in the areas of quality, productivity, and creativity. The challenge is to help teams adapt to change and still maintain a collaborative approach. This begins with helping individuals adapt to change while continuing to be effective.

If team member turnover is normal in your organization, take time to design a team structure that fits your culture. More and more organizations are gaining experience with forming and disbanding teams regularly as their business changes. People move on to new teams as needed. Using traditional team approaches in fast-changing environments can be risky. If teams are still a part of the culture, the task is to determine what elements of teamwork can be maintained. If teams can better perform the work, then the challenge is clear. Work with the teams, their coaches, and their leaders to help them adapt to, and support, the need for change.

CHAPTER 8

Global Teams

> **DEFINITION:** *Country-specific resources assigned to work collaboratively on a task to generate well-defined, global solutions, acceptable to the countries, cultures, and people affected. The group usually disbands when the task is complete. In other cases, the work of the group is ongoing.*

WHEN AN ORGANIZATION ESTABLISHES TEAMS with members of different nationalities, it must take everything it knows about teams and add in another major factor: cultural differences. Within any country, there are many cultural differences, yet the complexity increases significantly when team membership crosses country borders or continents. Whether this complexity is due to different languages, customs, beliefs, or values, the organization must understand and factor in these cultural differences as part of its development strategy for global teams.

For example, consider the experience of Hans Reuser, the senior training manager for Office Depot in the Netherlands. Office Depot operates from a value statement written by the U.S. headquarters' group, the European office leader from Belgium, and team members from Germany, England, Switzerland, and

Holland. Language differences make it more complex and complicate expressing thoughts and emotions. With this many nationalities, blending into one culture is a challenge. Teams must form from a mutual basis and shared purpose.

"GLOBAL TEAM SUCCESS COMES when you find people who are willing and able to work according to a value statement and truly live it. Then it doesn't matter if there are multiple nationalities. The values set the culture. And people either live it or leave. There is no room for lip service. There are a lot of differences between continents, countries, and thus between people. With respect, you can achieve a lot and build bridges."

— Hans Reuser, Senior Training Manager, Office Depot

How to best address global team issues is a challenge for most multinational organizations. They often find it difficult to figure out how and where to begin. The first order of business is to understand the cultures of the people you are asking to function as a team. Understanding the beliefs and values along with the various countries' histories can provide early insight into the group dynamics of a global team. This is accomplished through study, discussion, and experience.

FORMING THE GLOBAL TEAM

Once you understand the players, you need to focus on the basic building blocks of teamwork that cut across the involved cultures. The first challenge is to recognize the dynamics created by this particular combination of people. For example, if the mix includes Europeans or Asians, it is important to consider the cultures and histories of every country involved. Although Europeans and Asians share continents, it is a big mistake to treat the various countries as one culture or to ignore past conflicts or alliances. Add in players from North America, the Middle East, Africa, or South America, and the game becomes even more complex.

Often leaders strive to establish common ground for a global team by goal setting and stating a common, agreed-upon vision. This puts down a foundation for the team and allows it to maintain a task focus. To accomplish its goals, the team must be able to work interdependently to *do* the work. It is here that teams either find strength in their diversity or struggle with their team dynamics. By providing a strong base, the team has a better chance of successfully working on tasks and dealing with group dynamics and team issues as they arise.

There are predictable issues and challenges to be considered. Country governments, world history, and, inevitably, politics are real issues for global teams. By dealing with the things within the team's control and influencing what can be influenced, the team maximizes its impact. Accepting, acknowledging, and considering things outside of the team's control are also important.[1] We have already determined that teams are not right for every organization. Global teams can present an even bigger challenge than single-country teams.

Using the Global Team Feasibility Assessment shown in figure 8-1 can assist organizations in deciding to form a global team. Follow-up discussions can help the organization's leaders make business decisions to either use a global team approach or to find another method for organizing resources.

---

1. Morgan, *Navigating Cross-Cultural Ethics*, 1998.

Figure 8-1: Global Team Feasibility Assessment

Directions: Read each of the following questions and answer "yes" or "no." If the answer is "yes," describe what is in place that assures this item will not be a problem for the global team. If the answer is "no," determine if that item provides sufficient doubt for moving forward with forming a global team.

1. Are the top leaders from all countries fully supportive of this global team?
2. Can every country affected by this work be involved in the team?
3. Is the organization motivated to work on this task?
4. Can training and time bridge the cultural differences and result in true teamwork?
5. Can the project criteria be explained in a way that all team members can understand?
6. Is there sufficient funding to allow for travel and face-to-face sessions to build the team?
7. Are there clear deliverables and timelines to guide the team's work?
8. Has a team leader been identified who can guide this team's work?
9. Can a common language be spoken?
10. Can process resources be allocated to develop the team and assist in establishing effective team practices?

Scoring

Count the "yes" and "no" scores for each question from each decision-maker. For any item with "no" answers, discuss the item and reach agreement on whether or not it is sufficient reason to *not* form a global team.

GLOBAL TEAM DEVELOPMENT

Global teams can successfully approach and accomplish their tasks once cultural differences are acknowledged and accommodated. People of various cultures often have different styles of participation, ranging from assertive and direct to cautious and respectful.

These differences are frequently misunderstood. The risk of stereotyping and assuming intent can interfere with team progress.

In many global teams, it is likely that someone will be uncomfortable with brainstorming, open discussions, or unstructured problem-solving debates because in many cultures, hierarchy guides participation. Still, brainstorming should also be done, but within guidelines.

Figure 8-2: Brainstorming Guidelines

- Generate as many ideas as possible.
- Do not evaluate ideas: no idea is a bad idea.
- Give everyone an opportunity to share his or her ideas.
- Build on ideas to create additional ideas.
- Capture all ideas that are expressed.
- Keep going for as long as possible.
- Reassure everyone that all of their ideas are equal.

For example, in a team-building session involving Westerners and Koreans, I added several guidelines and norms to address cultural issues that inhibit Koreans from sharing ideas and opinions. In the Korean culture, it is customary to defer to individuals based on age, status, education, and authority of position. To set this custom aside, I requested that two norms be in place for this session. One was to leave all titles out in the hallway and to treat everyone equally during our discussions. The second norm was to have translation of all discussions occur during the discussions to allow for debate, questions, and agreements to be reached. Without addressing these two critical issues, the team building would have been limited.

Team building needs to be carefully designed with progressive steps that build on the group's success and expanding comfort level. As with any team, members gain the trust of others by recognizing and respecting the differences and compiling evidence that a teammate is trustworthy. The fundamentals of teamwork are the same across most borders and cultures. A shared vision with articulated values and goals helps set the necessary foundation for overcoming most differences. In tracking global team development, four phases can be observed as shown in figure 8-3.

In Phase 1, team members work separately and distinctly from each other and stay behind a mask of politeness. The cultural differences between the team members serve as a barrier that is accepted rather than challenged. The individual team members find ways to work independently from each other to perform their tasks. Direction comes from the leader. Little interaction occurs, and little understanding is gained.

Figure 8-3: Global Team Development Model

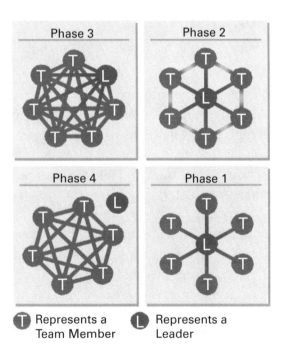

In Phase 2, time has helped team members begin developing relationships by talking to each other and exploring their differences. Potential sources of conflict become obvious, and areas of agreement lead to cooperation. With some cooperation, problem resolution across cultural boundaries and teamwork begins. The leader encourages the discussion and looks for opportunities to nurture teamwork, and the logical position or role for each team member begins to emerge.

During Phase 3, relationships are now in place and become stronger as teamwork becomes normalized as the way things are done. The team begins testing and perfecting its systems. Interdependence becomes a recognized way to do business. Cultural boundaries begin to blur as team members become comfortable with each other. The leader's role becomes that of a resource as the team moves toward self-management. Power and control issues surface and can get resolved because relationships are in place. Performance is the goal.

Finally, in Phase 4, the team is integrated and fully engaged, using teamwork to achieve its shared goals. Individual players are leveraged for their abilities. Cultural boundaries are either invisible or dissolved. Leadership sets direction, monitors performance, and provides assistance when asked. The results are maximized by the team's high level of performance and commitment to teamwork.

As part of global team development, time and energy must be devoted to gain an understanding of cultural differences. One area that must be discussed and resolved to avoid major disconnects as the team goes to work is how problems will be solved. Some people want to take a factual approach to problem solving. Others want to explore the people side of the situation. Then the question of proactiveness versus reactiveness comes into play, as does the level of risk the team is willing to assume. These aspects of problem solving, left unexplored, can bring teamwork to a standstill.

Figure 8-4 offers a simple assessment that can facilitate an open discussion and exploration of the similarities and differences in various team members.

Figure 8-4: Exploring Approaches to Problem Solving and Decision Making

Directions: *Consider your thought processes when facing a decision or solving a problem. On the following scale, circle the number that best represents your typical behavior. "When solving a problem or making a decision, I...":*

1	2	3	4
Avoid risks	Take small risks	Take medium risks	Take high risks

1	2	3	4
Focus on facts	Focus mostly on facts	Consider mostly impact on people	Focus on impact on people

1	2	3	4
React to the situation	Mostly react to the situation	Try to anticipate the situation	Predict and plan ahead

Using the results: Share your ratings with your teammates. Discuss similarities and differences. Reach agreements for addressing team problems and decisions in the areas of risk, facts versus people impact, and reactive versus proactive approaches.

CRITICAL ISSUES FACING GLOBAL TEAMS

A tremendous amount of creativity can result when groups of people come from a variety of settings. Once understood, unique differences and preferences can be exploited as part of the team's strength. Global teams can use their differences to discover the best way for them to function. This new way may differ significantly from typical ways we expect teams to work. And most times, this best way will be unique to the team itself and will not match any textbook description of teamwork.

The following sections of this chapter describe some key areas to manage and customize to fit the players on the team.

Communication

Language barriers cause some challenges in building global teams. Most organizations agree on a common business language, but that doesn't guarantee understanding. When team members have difficulty expressing their viewpoints, others have difficulty listening. This can be due to accents, word translation, or even the pace at which the team members are speaking the common language. Even without these issues, when people are listening in their second or third language, a message can be lost in the translation. Some important considerations in the area of communication include:

➤ Invest the necessary time and energy to reach common understanding during discussions.

➤ Explore and learn the differences in cultural nonverbal language.

➤ Choose language to match the formality of the situation.

➤ Show respect by learning phrases of each others' language.

➤ Seek to understand the beliefs and customs behind the stated messages.

➤ Allow time for informal discussion and translation, and take time for side conversations during important discussions.

➤ Use pre-reading to allow for comprehension and preparation.

➤ Set clear ground rules for discussions and presentations.

➤ Take regular and periodic breaks to give people a chance to think through the topics being discussed.

➤ Use a translator as necessary.

➤ Check accuracy of the translation.

➤ Offer language training in the agreed to business language.

Visuals

Language does not have to cause miscommunication if the team members are all aware of the challenges and compensate for language difficulties. Diagrams and drawings enhance understanding across languages, so using models, icons, graphics, and pictures in much greater proportion to words can assist common meaning and understanding. In working with global leadership teams, I have them draw the meaning of their value or belief statements. The discussion is rich, and the insights add to a deeper shared understanding of the phrases. Keys for using visuals include:

➤ Create models of all key concepts to reinforce the words.

➤ Capture key points of discussions and decisions in writing to avoid later disagreements.

➤ Strive to reach common definitions of terms.

➤ Provide advance copies of models for study and translation.

➤ Use visuals in meetings and discussions.

➤ Ask people to illustrate or sketch their ideas.

Creativity and Decision Making

Organization and team behavior differences are sometimes driven by the cultures of the team members' countries. These differences are fertile ground for misunderstanding and can lead to wasted time and hard feelings. The richness of differences and perspectives can become a source of wonderful solutions, but first the barriers around differences must be identified, and an appreciation of differences must be developed. What in one context could seem outrageous, in another context might be an innovative approach that solves a previously unsolvable problem.

For example, consider the experience of Lois Lukens, a General Motors international consultant, when she worked with a team that included both French and American members:

"THE PROJECT TEAM HAD TO REVISIT DECISIONS AND ACTIONS because follow up and follow through on agreements looked different in the two cultures. The issue could not be effectively addressed until the team learned that 'making a decision' means a different thing in France than in the United States. Because of their history and the French Revolution, when the French make a decision, they typically take it to the people it impacts and if the people think it's a good decision, they act. If not, they just do not do it . . . AND they do not come back to say that they are not intending to implement. In contrast, the Americans thought a decision was a commitment to act. Once this difference was surfaced, the team could put steps in the process to allow for additional involvement and communication of changes in direction."

— **Lois Lukens, Consultant, General Motors**

A team's ability to make good decisions is directly connected to its level of effectiveness. Some ways to increase the effectiveness of decision making include:

➤ Invest time to allow adequate discussion, idea exchange, and true dialogue.

➤ Explore team members' opinions, beliefs, and experiences with the process of decision making.

➤ Reach agreement on the best decision-making approach and process for this team and follow the process.

➤ Establish ground rules for sharing ideas and brainstorming.

➤ Monitor agreements and seek explanation when things "go wrong."

Inclusion

Teams with a majority of members from a common country have a greater risk of leaving out the minority members. The team tends to hear the familiar members and exclude, often unintentionally, the different voices. If the leader is in the minority, these dynamics can change, although the majority may still find ways to work independently and talk in their small group to plan their strategies. Key to addressing these potentially destructive cliques are processes that monitor equality of participation. These processes should include polling each member for opinions, agreement, or concerns.

Bridging the communication and cultural barriers requires a significant time and effort investment. Finding opportunities to include a variety of team members can help address issues of exclusion. Some examples to consider:

➤ Treat every team member with respect and professionalism.

➤ Monitor levels of involvement and participation to identify and correct inequities.

➤ Be aware of past antagonism between countries to avoid triggering past disagreements.

➤ Find areas of common interest to share within the group.

➤ Use food and drink to facilitate cross-cultural appreciation.

➤ Adjust the speed and length of conversations to the group's ability to work in a common language.

➤ Organize social and work events to increase time spent getting to know one another.

Commonalities

Although there are certainly differences to manage, there are also common characteristics that facilitate teamwork. Most people want to be successful, have effective relationships, learn and grow, and perform meaningful work. These drivers can be tapped to align people. Having individual high standards for achievement helps teams reach high levels of team performance. With a shared drive to achieve, people signal their willingness to take on and conquer challenges. Achievement usually aligns with high-quality outcomes. Sharing responsibility and accountability for achieving goals can erase most cultural differences.

Teams must be motivated to perform. This motivation often requires alignment to a goal. Global teams must share a vision and goals and commit to work together to succeed. Once the goal is clear and agreed to, the language spoken should be of no consequence. Leaders of global teams must help keep the team aligned and achieving its goals.

Making sure that everyone's efforts count and that each member contributes to the success of the whole builds a true team. Distractions caused by cultural or language differences must be noted and addressed. Leaders must set realistic yet challenging goals for the team, encourage risk-taking, and show enthusiasm for team progress. Building relationships requires an authentic interest in other people. It combines both concern for others and an appreciation of the talents each brings to the team. To build effective relationships, a person starts by understanding and accepting his or her own strengths and weaknesses. Then people must accept others for who they are. This acceptance allows team members to grow and allows the team to leverage each member's strengths.

Focusing energy on building strong relationships has many benefits. It creates an environment more open to risk-taking and honesty. The team's energy can be directed to the task at hand rather than being concerned with other team issues. Strong relationships transcend cultural differences. When people are sensitive to each other's needs, they can address issues quickly. Through their relationships, the team gathers knowledge and grows its level of understanding. Team members must listen and ask questions to learn about each individual on the team.

Learning and growth often translate directly into satisfaction. Most people feel happiest when they are learning new things and increasing their capabilities. Encouraging the team to accept responsibility for the team's performance is one way to spur this growth. When a new global team is formed, the opportunities to learn are countless. The first major opportunity for learning comes from exploring the differences in each team member's experiences. The next is turning the differences into the team's strength. Looking at the team's task from the various viewpoints can provide extraordinary insight. This insight can energize and inspire creativity and breakthrough thinking and learning, as shown in figure 8-5. In this circle of learning, the core is the knowing zone—built from all our experiences and knowledge. The second ring is the learning zone, where new experiences help create new understanding and possibly skills. The outer ring is the breakthrough thinking zone—where we stretch, take risks, and open up to new knowledge and insights. Key behaviors that promote learning are maintaining a positive outlook, being curious about people and things, having success, gaining skills through practice, and building supportive relationships. Limiters are fear, narrow-minded thinking, and win-lose relationships.

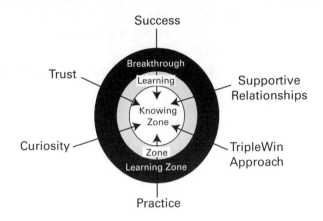

Figure 8-5: Circle of Learning

©TripleWin Consulting LLC, used with permission.

Meaningful work is at the root of motivation. On a global level, recognizing the criteria for measuring the meaningfulness is important. What may seem essential to one person may seem insignificant to another. Again, understanding the cultural elements of work comes into play. Most people work tirelessly for a cause they believe in. The challenge may come in the form of how the work is done. For example, consider the experience of Joe LoCicero, a Harley-Davidson consultant:

"I HAD THE OPPORTUNITY TO WORK ON A GLOBAL TASK TEAM in Argentina. The leadership team consisted of several Brazilians, several Argentines, a Briton, a couple of North Americans (I was taught by the South Americans that saying "American" is not specific enough), a Portuguese, and several Germans. One simple dynamic that frustrated the Germans and the Briton was the South American sense of time. Business meetings did not start on time. The Germans were early to meetings while the Briton and North Americans were on time. And the South Americans were late and wondered what, in the grand scheme of things, was the big deal about being exact. In addition, decision-making for the Germans was data driven, and decisions for the South Americans placed more weight on people. The South Americans expect all leaders to show the appropriate regard for people."

— Joe LoCicero, Consultant, Harley-Davidson

As the world's global boundaries continue to be crossed, many nationalities are gaining experience from being on global teams. For many people, working in international teams is the first move outside of the norms of their own country. This lack of experience results in a real naïveté toward anything other than the way things are done at home. In preparation for global teamwork, the following activities would benefit most individuals:

➤ Attend meaningful cultural training to learn about your teammates.

➤ Be considerate and accommodating to other time zones.

➤ Travel outside your country often to get an understanding of how the rest of the world functions and how different countries perceive your country.

➤ Learn to speak a few words in other languages (hello, good-bye, please, and thank you will suffice); even if you have a poor accent, trying earns trust, confidence, and goodwill.

➤ Consider the cultural aspects of *every* country, not just by continent.

➤ Be empathic not only to different emotions but also to different cultural habits.

➤ If you do not understand the differences, ask and listen to the advice of the people who do.

➤ Try to understand and respond to the culture, norms, and needs of other teammates, and respect their right to disagree with your way of thinking.

➤ Make decisions based on appropriate global criteria and perspectives, not just from your own point of view.

➤ Acknowledge experience and knowledge gaps in areas of expertise of the business between countries.

➤ Share insights and suggestions when working with people of other cultures.

➤ Be patient and listen more than you speak to truly appreciate the differences in cultures.

➤ Speak slowly.

➤ Remember that team and trust building require patience and sensitivity.

➤ Pay attention to the little things—e.g., how you dress, when you drink your coffee, when you eat your meals; also, try new foods, show curiosity about the country, culture, and even holiday customs of team members from other countries.

➤ Learn about the country's habits and follow them when visiting a foreign team member's country.

➤ Balance country pride with respect and curiosity of other countries' points of view.

➤ Be natural, be yourself, yet be sensitive and open to learning about others, reaching out to other team members in friendship.

CONCLUSION

The approach you take with global teammates matters greatly. If you simply tolerate the differences and try to get others to think like you do, you erase the biggest benefit of global teamwork: the differences. Country to country, differences in life experiences can unleash new ideas and new approaches to global challenges. It takes patience and true openness of minds and behaviors to generate global synergy.

I designed and delivered a team-building program off-site to twenty top executives (ten Westerners from the United Kingdom, Australia, and the United States and ten South Koreans) in South Korea. One activity had the Westerners and Koreans in separate groups, answering the following three questions:

What would you like the other group to begin doing?

What would you like the other group to continue doing?

What would you like the other group to stop doing?

The exchange of information and the resulting dialogue were outstanding. The responses opened up a much needed line of communication. Understandings grew, relationships moved forward, and changes were agreed to on-the-spot.

With English often designated as the common language, U.S., Canadian, Australian, British, and other English-speaking teammates may have an advantage. That advantage is quickly erased, however, if the language barrier is not overcome, so that all global players can make a full contribution to the team's efforts. Going beyond the language to understand the cultures of your teammates' countries can be a rich and rewarding experience. Accurate translation and assuring shared understanding, although time consuming and sometimes painful, should never be rushed or sacrificed.

The roles you play in global teams can be the same as the ones you assume in natural work teams or project teams. Focus on the task at hand while growing and maintaining group effectiveness. In addition, accept responsibility for maximizing the benefits of having a global perspective. The world in many ways is getting smaller. Technology has increased the world's access to knowledge and information. Global awareness leads to better decision making if you consciously and openly embrace it. The approach you take in tackling business problems as teams can set an example for the world.

CHAPTER 9

Executive Leadership Teams

> DEFINITION: *A group of top managers who are peers; the person to whom they commonly report is usually the president, CEO, or general manager. This team is typically responsible for providing strategic direction to the organization.*

THE IMPORTANCE OF AN EFFECTIVE SENIOR TEAM of an organization should not be underestimated. An executive leadership team is usually composed of successful, smart, hardworking executives who have been effective in their own domains. However, there are unique challenges facing each executive when they make the transition from being the "boss" of their own domains to being an equal member of a team. Teamwork is not always natural to these executives. Team behaviors require team skills such as listening, collaborative problem solving, and decision making. The skills and appreciation of collaboration are so important they are now being taught in MBA and other executive development programs.

Having a team in place at the top of an organization is counter to most organizational structures. This makes clarifying the

operating norms and procedures critical so that everyone understands his or her role and knows the rules. The first order of business is to determine if there is a legitimate need for the executives
to function as a team. Business complexity certainly suggests that
it is difficult for one leader to provide adequate direction. Still,
executive leadership teams are not naturally teams at all, but usually a collection of people heading functional departments reporting to the top leader. The determining factors for the need of an
executive leadership team are how the leader structures the work
to be done and the degree of interdependence that exists.

So when should an executive leadership team be established?
Any time there is an environment open to collaboration and teamwork. I have seen this most often in times of major change, such
as reorganization or implementation of a key business strategy.
This is when synergy and shared ownership are absolutely essential. Then even the toughest executives see the value of teamwork. The biggest challenge for executive leadership teams is
defining the shared responsibilities.

In general, when an organization decides to use a matrix structure, having an executive leadership team to provide coordination and direction is a major benefit. A matrix structure typically
requires multiple reporting relationships, often due to project assignments combined with functional responsibilities.[1] This structure creates a balance of power among the project and functional
leaders so that neither the project nor the functional goals become more important. Matrix structures usually optimize the use
of resources and expertise, making them ideal for challenging
times. When properly managed by an executive leadership team,
this structure improves communication, increases organizational
flexibility, and allows for creative problem solving. The executive
leadership team must provide coordination and clear accountability. Without it, matrix structures often deteriorate into conflict
and power struggles, and the benefits are quickly erased.

---

1. McShane and Von Glinow, *Organizational Behavior,* 2000.

Real teams do real work. The executives cannot just meet to listen to presentations to review policy and strategy options or to set general direction as a working committee. Their work must have a minimum level of interdependence. Then the executive leadership team's issues are essentially the same as in other teams: who has the most power and influence, who has what role, how is conflict managed, how do decisions get made, and how is work distributed. The risks are bigger, so the game is played harder, but the issues are the same or similar to those of other teams.

When there is *not* a legitimate need for a team, but the leader and/or the executives believe that they should be a team, strange things can happen. The decision is made to function as a team, but work continues to be done along independent, functional lines. The natural behaviors are autonomy and independent decision making. When confronted with their lack of team-like behavior, changes are prescribed, and team-like behaviors are expected with everyone committing to follow team norms and purpose. This creates two levels of functioning: a public one, where the group members put on the mask of teamwork, and a private one, which reflects the reality of the situation. This inconsistency can create uncertainty and insecurity, and the politics of the group can intensify and result in destructive behavior. The irony is that by demanding team-like behavior, the opposite is accomplished. This is not the case when forming a team to manage the enterprise is appropriate and useful. However, some of the same challenges still arise.

There are critical components for successful executive leadership teams. By examining the practices of actual executive leadership teams, these elements can be clearly identified. Once identified, establishing a strong foundation and providing feedback to the team are essential to long-term viability. In working with various executive leadership teams, I have found specific examples of things that work well and things that derail the team. The following three examples are actual situations. The key lessons that are derived from these situations have global application.

CASE STUDY #1

The Cost of Conflict Avoidance

A top executive had a wonderful ability to build alliances. He made friends, built credibility, and established trust quickly. He was inclusive, and he openly encouraged different ways of thinking. This strength became a weakness, however, when keeping peace became a bigger priority than helping his executive leadership team surface and resolve conflicts. As often happens, a key strength that is overused can turn into a major weakness. There were warning signs that can serve as lessons for other executive team leaders:

1. The team leader had eighteen direct reports and traveled about 50 percent of the time. Not much time had been invested in developing the team, and many of the executives on the team were young and inexperienced. The individual executives stumbled along because they had little or no one-on-one time with their leader.

2. He avoided any conflict that might damage alliances and relationships. Any disagreements that surfaced in team meetings were redirected to off-line discussions and decision making.

3. The rest of the organization saw the executive leadership team as ineffective. And because the norm in that organization was conflict avoidance, this issue could not be addressed openly.

4. Meetings were information-sharing forums instead of a meeting place for meaningful dialogue and debate. Attendance was irregular, and substitutes were sent to "fill the seats." The group was too large to have meaningful discussions, and debate was discouraged. To compensate for meeting ineffectiveness, the top executive often pulled together half-hour strategy meetings with four key leaders on an as-needed basis. The other thirteen

members felt alienated by this group. The larger executive leadership team was undermined, and an "us versus them" environment developed.

5. Decisions were often unsupported or failed to be implemented because people were not aligned. The corporate head nod became the norm, which meant "I heard you, but I will do what I think is best once I leave this room." Often it took a crisis to trigger a decision and strong champions to see that it was implemented.

KEY LESSONS

➤ In executive teams, eight to twelve members allow for relationships to mature and for discussions to be balanced.

➤ The contribution of various team members is severely limited without investing time in exploring differences.

➤ Disagreements are a healthy part of a team's culture. They create energy, insight, and creativity when constructively managed.

➤ When meetings are the key mechanism for a team to function, the meeting agenda *must* engage the participants in a meaningful way.

➤ Define the decision-making process and follow it religiously.

CASE STUDY #2

What Are the Rules?

Along with her appointment as president, this executive inherited an existing executive leadership team. She was pleased to discover that this team had a written set of meeting norms, along with a regular meeting schedule. On the wall, framed, was the following list of meeting norms:

➤ Start meetings on time

➤ One person talks at a time

➤ Focus on the current topic being discussed

➤ Be flexible to others' ideas

➤ Do not be defensive

➤ Respect others

➤ Express your opinions

➤ Agree to disagree

➤ Use "ditto" (i.e., do not repeat stated points of view)

➤ End the meeting as friends

➤ Celebrate the wins

➤ Conclude the meeting on time

In addition, the executive leadership team followed a consensus decision-making model to ensure full support and commitment to all decisions. Before finalizing any decision, the team members used small flags to signal their positions: green meant fully supportive, yellow meant some additional discussion was needed, and red meant major issues remained unresolved. The norm was until everyone was "green," there was no decision.

Armed with these tools, this executive leadership team was set up to have successful meetings. However, in reality, this team struggled with decisions and functioned more like a group or committee of individual executives. After one year of tolerating marginal results, the president made major changes in the team meetings and turned the group into a functional team. Here's what she did:

1. She created a strategic plan that required each of the thirteen team members (who represented different functional areas) to report quarterly; this plan was intended to increase interdependence among team members. Many of the plans were cross-functional. This maintained high involvement in the meetings and increased the level of working knowledge among functional areas.

2. Because the weekly meetings did not create the level of interaction and collaboration the new president wanted, she instituted daily thirty-minute teleconference calls, with required attendance and follow-up assignments.

3. She no longer permitted substitutes to attend the weekly meetings. She noted absences and required members to seek prior approval to miss a meeting. She accepted only reasonable excuses.

4. She added a strategic planner to the group to track discussions, decisions, and assignments.

5. After painful sessions, she asked each individual to describe how he or she was feeling. Although this discussion was entered into with reluctance, having this discussion allowed team members to express their feelings.

6. She revised the meeting norms and used her strong team development and meeting skills to guide the group.

KEY LESSONS

➤ A good team leader makes sure everyone understands the team's norms and both the formal and informal norms of behavior: i.e., how they *really* work, not just what is said or written on paper. For instance, if we say we will make decisions by consensus, is that what really happens? If not, everyone waits for the boss to decide so they can be on the right side of the decision.

➤ Interdependence and a working knowledge across the boundaries of the various functional areas must be built. Members of executive leadership teams must be able to wear a company hat to address big issues.

➤ Strategic and tactical issues belong on an executive leadership team's agenda, delegating operational matters to functional areas.

➤ Having meetings as often as necessary circumvents decision making without team involvement. A key to team success is striving for consensus and alignment on all critical decisions.

➤ Norms should trigger desirable behaviors. Take them off the wall when they are no longer appropriate, or modify them when necessary.

➤ Invest time to develop personal relationships between team members. Without relationships, there is no team.

➤ Track implementation of decisions and action items to instill discipline and accountability within the team.

➤ A meeting assessment tool helps monitor the team's meeting effectiveness (see figure 9-2 for a sample). Use the results of the assessment with the team to identify changes they want to make.

Figure 9-2. Executive Leadership Team Meeting Assessment

Directions: *For periodic review of meeting effectiveness, have each member complete the following assessment.*

---

1. How often do we stay on track with the agenda, including time for each item?

1	2	3	4	5	6	7	8	9	10

Never   Rarely   Sometimes   Usually   Always

Comments:

---

2. How often is the overall quality of our discussions high?

1	2	3	4	5	6	7	8	9	10

Never   Rarely   Sometimes   Usually   Always

Comments:

---

3. Would you rate the overall quality of information presented as high?

1	2	3	4	5	6	7	8	9	10

Never   Rarely   Sometimes   Usually   Always

Comments:

---

4. How often are the correct topics getting on the agenda?

1	2	3	4	5	6	7	8	9	10

Never   Rarely   Sometimes   Usually   Always

Comments:

---

5. Do we spend an appropriate amount of time on agenda items?

1	2	3	4	5	6	7	8	9	10

Never   Rarely   Sometimes   Usually   Always

Comments:

CHARACTERISTICS OF AN EFFECTIVE EXECUTIVE TEAM LEADER

Every team needs strong leadership, especially an executive leadership team where the egos are big and the stakes are high. When the top executive does not have the skills to develop and lead a team, the results of the team can be severely limited. Forming a cadre of leaders to share responsibility can help. Just as teaming a strong administrator with a visionary brings both skills to the organization, the same is true for bringing in a skilled team builder. The success of the team rests with the top leader, along with the executives on the team who combine their skills and commit to making a team approach work.

True business leaders guide from within a team, see different points of view, and then help the group arrive at solutions that integrate individual ideas and eventually result in the organization moving forward. Integration of individual points of view works better than domination, coercion, or even compromise in getting a decision made or a job done. The skills of most top executives are put to the test in leading an executive leadership team. However, without strong leadership, executive leadership teams falter in times of change, and without teamwork, every decision is vulnerable to each individual player's agenda. The success of most executive leadership teams rests on the shoulders of their leaders.

Credit or criticism of an executive leadership team's performance also falls on the leader. The leader's behavior sets the tone of the team. Their expectations and follow-through affect the results in many ways. This is not an easy role. Being a strong executive is not enough. Successfully building, nurturing, and maintaining a team of high-powered executives takes most, if not all, of the characteristics shown in figure 9-1.

Figure 9-1: Necessary Characteristics of Executive Team Leaders

Characteristic: Facilitative Style
Actions: Achieve results through others; encourage discussions, collaboration, and debates; recognize team results to nurture a team approach; require information sharing across groups.

Characteristic: Strategic Thinker
Actions: Strive for alignment; explore the vision, mission, and organizational direction; keep the pieces linked together; articulate the big picture; link team to other organizations or environmental situations to drive alignment across the organization; create a vision and strategy for the organization.

Characteristic: Business Focused
Actions: Focus on measurable results; build interdependence and teamwork; reward performance.

Characteristic: Results Oriented
Actions: Demand results to get results; implement plans and monitor performance; delve below the surface to get to the root cause; explore various angles to trigger meaningful discussion and debate; set direct, clear expectations; take personal responsibility for initiating change.

Characteristic: Skilled Communicator ·
Actions: Initiate and prompt discussions; encourage dialogue; facilitate debates; spend meeting time wisely; "stir the pot" if necessary to flush out disagreements; evaluate team membership.

Characteristic: Relationship Driven
Actions: Show care for the members of the team; use a personal touch with the other leaders; create strong relationships and a foundation of trust; encourage learning and risk-taking; stimulate a team's growth; trust and empower others.

Characteristic: Sense of Urgency
Actions: Balance impatience with high quality standards; do the right things right; model a sense of urgency; create energy in others to generate outstanding results; refuse to protect the status quo; institute continuous improvement as an operating value.

Characteristic: Alignment
Actions: Engage individuals until issues are worked out; connect the need for change with performance goals and organizational structure; make messages clear to people in terms they can understand and relate to, no matter what their managerial level or background.

Characteristic: Tough Love
Actions: Confront nonperformance and incompetence; find ways to bring out an individual team member's greatness; supplement one member's weakness with another member's strength.

Helping others grow and achieve results is a key responsibility of an executive team leader. Encouraging discussion and collaboration and recognizing the team's performance nurtures a team approach. Being the lead strategist for the team means helping the team articulate the big picture. Linking the team to other organizations or the overall business drives alignment. Executive team leaders must avoid focusing all their energy into one or two specific areas of the business. Instead, they must help their teams look across the functions and build interdependence and teamwork. Demanding results is critical to getting results. Maintaining and communicating the appropriate sense of urgency can lead to focus and timely results.

If one person knows all the answers, you do not need a team. Having meaningful discussions justifies having people invest their time in meetings. If a team becomes complacent, the leader needs to challenge the members and shake up the status quo. If members are not contributing, the leader must evaluate and determine whether they need to be on the team.

Leadership and teamwork are all about relationships. Building authentic, caring relationships allows business to be conducted in a win-win environment. Conflicts can be healthy and constructive, and energy can be generated through healthy debate. Balancing demands with consideration is a requirement. These characteristics are not taught in business schools or in many organizations, yet they are proven to help create a successful team environment. Team-based cultures do not have to be limited to the lowest levels of an organization. It is possible to build an effective senior leadership team. One solution is to avoid the traps that have led other executive leadership teams to yield disappointing results.

COMMON TRAPS TO AVOID

Along with selecting and developing the team of executives, effectively handling mistakes is essential. In examining many executive leadership teams, the following common mistakes have derailed most teams at one time or another.

Working on the Wrong Things: Leadership teams often work on the wrong things. They find themselves driven more by urgency than by the importance of issues. They spend most of their time on managerial issues and short-change setting direction and leading the organization. They plan and budget, deal with people issues, and solve operational problems. In addition, they need to be creating the future direction of the company, outlining strategies, and aligning and mobilizing people.

Public Floggings: In an executive leadership team environment, the ability to discuss problems is important. However, when an individual or individuals are singled out and criticized in front of the team, some members interpret that as punishment for risk-taking. Or, if a team member takes the initiative to expose a problem and is chastised for it, the reputation of "killing the messenger" decreases the likelihood of open discussion in the future. Discussions must be held out in the open and focused on bringing about organizational success.

Impatience: Wanting to involve the team yet wanting to control the outcome and wanting things right now are often in conflict with a team style of management. Teams require time and processes to solve problems and make decisions. The leader who takes back legitimate assignments that belong to the team disempowers the team.

Poor Decision Processes: Most executive leadership teams struggle with making decisions. This problem stems from a combination of poor decision-making *processes* and inadequate *skills* in group decision making. Team decision-making does not have to mean delays, pain, and hours of debate. Having a bottom-line discipline, clear process guidelines, and strong relationships can pave the way to smooth, effective decisions. Doing necessary pre-work can help avoid unproductive discussion. Lacking these things, decision-making sessions can be chaotic, ineffective, and a waste of time.

Ego Conflicts: Executives rise to their positions based on skill, achievement, and talent. Expecting them to leave their egos at the door and to function as a peer group with equal authority is often a big stretch. Best results are achieved when the group members have at least a perceived balance of power. Without some balance, no matter what the issue, the high-power members will control the discussions and the final outcomes.

Competition Versus Collaboration: When the executives see themselves as competitors for resources or the next promotion, teamwork gets in the way. Ambition and egos can be so strong at the executive level that it is impossible to generate true collaboration. The ultimate goal is to enable every executive on the team to have a role in setting and implementing the strategic direction of the company through genuine teamwork with other executives. An interactive executive team can generate synergy and enable the organization to adapt faster to customer demands and competitive threats.

Resistance to Change: Long-standing groups or members of high seniority can develop an immune system to new ideas, practices, and people. Left unchallenged, resistance wins over progress and innovation.

CASE STUDY #3

Add in the Complication of Politics

Many examples of these common traps can be found in a senior union-management team of a large manufacturing complex. The biggest challenges have been changing membership on the leadership team, organizational and union politics, and dealing with huge competitive challenges. Taking on any one of these challenges is a major task. But balancing all three simultaneously strained the capability of this executive leadership team.

A real challenge for most executive leadership teams is debating with each other, expressing disagreement with each other's actions in a constructive manner and still being able to make the best value decision for the situation. This is often difficult when there are different levels of leaders within the team or when the team is a combination of union and management leaders. However, without the ability to speak honestly within the team, it is difficult, if not impossible, to make high-quality decisions.

Few events can tear down the morale of a team more than to invest in reaching a decision or recommendation and then have it overturned by someone on the team, someone outside the team, or a leader acting independently. Changing the team's decision or ignoring recommendations can destroy the team's motivation. Here were the specific problems that this team faced:

1. Turnover of key members occurred often and kept the group in the forming stage. As each new member joined, the team needed to recreate itself, including revisiting norms and clarifying its purpose.

2. The team struggled with establishing a clear purpose and appropriate membership. Even after decisions on membership were agreed to, membership issues continued to be raised.

3. The team struggled with taking on the tough issues because cultural, political, and environmental pressures were intense.

4. No agreement existed for in-bounds and out-of-bounds behaviors in meetings or in daily interactions. Norms were not enough because commitment and discipline were missing.

KEY LESSONS

➤ The top leaders are key: their behaviors influence the openness and level of teamwork that occurs. Addressing inappropriate behavior of members is one way to maintain team decorum. One player can spoil the team if inappropriate behavior goes unaddressed and uncorrected.

➤ Clearly agreeing on the task at hand and defining a fair process for decision making is an essential first step in team decision making. Honoring decisions is critical once agreements are reached. Steps in decision making include implementation and follow-through. Revisiting decisions calls into question the effectiveness of not just the process, but the team as well.

➤ Punishing team members for expressing unpopular opinions can stimulate risk-averse behavior. Playing it safe becomes a consideration in everyone's approach.

➤ Balancing cultural, political, and technical agendas takes time and skill. Ignoring them does not make them go away.

➤ Avoid mixing politics and management as much as possible.

CONCLUSION

Unfortunately, many executive leadership teams eventually fail in their pursuit of team effectiveness. For some, long before they are disbanded or reorganized, there is frustration and fatigue among members. The core problem is that no matter how good the concept sounds as the executive leadership team is formed, this type of team often evolves into a committee making mostly operational decisions and actually causing the organization to wait for them to discuss and decide.

Executive leadership teams are best suited for strategic planning, not for running the daily business. The goal is to make operational decisions easier for the rest of the organization. Alignment comes from clear vision and direction. This is the key contribution of the top leader. Chaos comes from having the wrong players involved in various daily activities. Selecting the right members of the executive leadership team, providing education and exposure to a strategic planning process, and insisting on having discipline for strategy development is essential. With these, an executive leadership team has the foundation for success.

Paying attention to the health of the executive leadership team is critical. Issues surfaced and dealt with in a timely manner benefit the entire organization. Figure 9-3 offers an assessment tool to help make this evaluation. Use the data to work with the team to identify, plan, and implement changes. An annual assessment may be the key to long-term executive team health.

Figure 9-3: Executive Leadership Team Assessment

Directions: *To evaluate your executive leadership team's health, complete the following assessment by circling the number that most accurately describes typical team meetings or problem-solving sessions. Total the numbers circled and refer to the scoring information for a general assessment of your team's health.*

1. Decision Making

1	2	3	4	5

Process is undefined; top leader makes most of the decisions.

Well-defined process, with high level of involvement by members.

2. Meeting Format

1	2	3	4	5

Meetings are focused on presentations, and discussions are polite and orderly.

Dialogue and debate create high energy and raise new issues.

3. Conflict

1	2	3	4	5

Conflict is discouraged and handled one-on-one, not during the team meeting.

Conflict is used to stimulate discussion of key topics during the team meeting.

4. Relationships

1	2	3	4	5

Win-lose relationships are allowed to exist; inappropriate behavior goes unaddressed.

Win-win relationships are developed and nurtured by spending time building trust.

5. Accountability

1	2	3	4	5

Little to no follow-up or review of decisions or actions is completed.

Decisions and action steps are monitored and tracked.

Figure 9-3: Executive Leadership Team Assessment

6. Strategy

1	2	3	4	5

Strategy is limited to annual business plan discussions and when new situations require it.

Strategic items are discussed on a regular basis as the primary team and meeting focus.

7. Top Leader

1	2	3	4	5

Top leader sets the tone as his/her meeting and usually talks first and most often in key discussions.

Leadership and accountability are shared; top leader models effective team member behaviors.

8. Balanced Participation

1	2	3	4	5

Top leader and a few other members control the discussion and drive decisions and actions.

Every person on the team plays an active part and makes a meaningful contribution.

Scoring

8-16   Little or no structure is in place for an executive leadership team. Some structure exists to function as a committee or staff of the top executive. Evaluate the need for teamwork and make necessary changes to create a team environment or accept the role of executive committee.

17-25   Some structure for an executive leadership team is in place. Areas with scores of 2 or below must be addressed to reach high performance while building on areas that score 3 and above. With additional effort, an effective executive leadership team can be built.

26-40   Most of the structure for high performance is in place. Monitoring actual results and maintaining the right relationships are critical to sustain a high level of teamwork. Assimilate new team members to avoid regression. Any score below 3 needs to be examined and addressed.

CHAPTER 10

Conclusion

TODAY'S ORGANIZATIONS HAVE MANY CHALLENGES AND OPPOR-TUNITIES. As competition continues to escalate, doing more with less becomes the rule of the day. Running parallel to this is the need for organizations to provide opportunities for employees to learn, to be challenged, to have meaningful work, and to have a sense of belonging. So, how do we get there? One step at a time.

Organizations must examine their uniqueness, explore their history, understand their present situation, and describe their desired future. The key leaders must use their best judgment to determine how to get the job done. I truly believe teams can be an effective structure. There is debate around teams versus groups or collaborative workplaces. Even around whether what I call a team fits the theoretical definition. To these debates, I say, if it works, do it. Call it what best fits for the situation. Adapt and be flexible. Keep your options open.

In writing *The Driving Force*, I looked at the variety of ways teams work. Team theory was a useful guide, but I know there is an exception to every rule. I love finding the exceptions and pushing for doing what works. Today we all need to be focused problem solvers who know what questions to ask and who are committed to act on those answers. As a result of asking the right questions, teams can be directed to work on the right things with the right level of involvement of others. When we encourage people to ask questions, they gain understanding. And with that understanding, we have a chance to move forward.

Work teams often demand more change than many managers are willing to accept. Because teams require a sharing of power and information, they threaten the traditional power structure. Every team needs a manager who gets people excited about achieving their goals. Team members do the work, but team managers help set goals, make plans, give feedback on performance, follow up, and create a strong sense of motivation. Managers need to encourage dialogue, create challenges to inspire the team's creativity, and provide the resources to allow the team to produce value-added results.

Team managers must stay involved and be flexible with their approach and style. When a team needs structure and specific instructions, the leader must provide them. When a team needs hands-on coaching, the leader must have the ability to provide that as well. And when a team is ready to function autonomously, leaders must be ready to provide the necessary resources and independence.

Leaders must be developed to create and nurture teams. As a leader's responsibilities change to align with a team structure, skills to perform these new tasks must be taught. Knowledge and skills in empowerment, coaching, team development, and facilitation are essential for leaders of high-performance teams. The ultimate goal is to help leaders who were developed in a power-control-directive style organization to modify their approach. At the same time, business skills must be taught to the teams to equip them for making sound business decisions as they take on managing their teams and businesses.

Teams should never be unmanaged, yet they must be managed differently than individuals. Depending on the maturity of the team, involvement by the leader should vary. New teams should have extensive direction from leaders. As the teams mature, more independence and authority can be granted as long as the team's performance warrants increased autonomy. This is true at both the individual and team level.

Why use teams? Because they work. Are they worth the effort? If you are not sure, do more investigation. Teams are not easy and they are not free. But when managed and led properly, teams pay for themselves in creativity, flexibility, and organizational commitment. And in these challenging times, a strong team may be the difference between being just good enough or being really great.

Is your organization ready to successfully use teams? The Organization Assessment (figure 10-1) can help determine just how ready you are or, maybe more importantly, what you can do to be successful with teams.

Figure 10-1: Organization Assessment

Directions: *For each of the strategies listed below, circle the word(s) that best describe how much this particular strategy is in place within your organization today.*

1. Shared and flexible leadership roles

Not At All   Somewhat   Totally

2. Individual and mutual accountability

Not At All   Somewhat   Totally

3. Interrelated performance measures

Not At All   Somewhat   Totally

4. Open information sharing

Not At All   Somewhat   Totally

5. Collaborative problem solving

Not At All   Somewhat   Totally

6. Shared commitment to goal(s)

Not At All   Somewhat   Totally

7. Full use of individual members' knowledge

Not At All   Somewhat   Totally

8. Active participation in decision making

Not At All   Somewhat   Totally

9. Experimentation, innovation, and creativity

Not At All   Somewhat   Totally

10. Honest, trusting relationships

Not At All   Somewhat   Totally

Figure 10-1: Organization Assessment

Scoring

Each of these strategies plays a key role in supporting teams within an organization. Any item receiving a rating less than "Totally" must be examined to determine if it will be an inhibiting force to the successful use of teams. If it is not possible for the entire organization to implement these strategies, it is essential for the area the team functions in to have these characteristics.

Section III
Team Toolkit

IMPLEMENTING STRONG TEAM PROCESSES TAKES TIME AND EF-FORT. This toolkit provides activities to strengthen the H.E.A.R.T. of a team:

➤ Enhance *honest dialogue* between team members and their leaders.

➤ Increase the *effectiveness* of meetings and problem solving.

➤ Increase *accountability* by providing a framework of team norms to allow for ongoing success.

➤ Improve *respectful relationships* by building understanding and *trust*.

The first part of this toolkit features some exercises to help facilitate productive, effective, and efficient teamwork:

1. Team bingo

2. Team norms

3. Meeting tools: a team meeting assessment, a meeting facilitator skills checklist, and a meeting feedback checklist

4. The TripleWin relationship assessment

5. The trust continuum

6. Passing the baton—changing leaders

7. Assimilating new team members

8. Continuous improvement at warp speed

In addition, the second part of this toolkit features the assessments presented in the earlier chapters. Assessing a team's health is essential. As we know with our own health, we are instructed to check with our doctor before beginning any strenuous exercise. He or she checks for general health before suggesting any changes. Assessments perform the same function. Accurately diagnosing what interventions a team needs is the critical first step in every case.

The assessments help identify the key information needed by the team, team leader, or any resource working to assist a team increase its effectiveness. When used properly, either one-on-one in an interview setting with team and organization members or as part of a team event, the following tools help organizations and teams identify important next steps:

1. **Organizational Readiness Assessment:
    Are You Ready to Use Teams?**
    How and Why to Use: Use this assessment with leaders to determine their organization's level of readiness for using teams. Each question defines a key area that must be addressed to assure teams have the support structure required for them to work effectively.

2. **Great Team Player Characteristics**
    How and Why to Use: Use as part of a team skills training course or a team-building event. It allows participants to do a self-assessment of their own behaviors and identify areas needing improvement.

3. **Team Effectiveness Assessment**
    How and Why to Use: Use this assessment with existing teams (new or old) in either a team meeting or during a team-building event to identify areas of team effectiveness that need to be improved.

4. **Project Team Readiness Assessment**
    How and Why to Use: Use this assessment to describe your organization and to determine readiness to implement

and support a project team approach.

5. **Virtual Team Attributes Self-Assessment**
   How and Why to Use: Use this assessment with individuals to help them assess their suitability for virtual work.

6. **Quick-Change Team Assessment**
   How and Why to Use: Use this assessment with individuals to determine their readiness to be a member of a quick-change team.

7. **Global Team Feasibility Assessment**
   How and Why to Use: Use this assessment with leaders to determine the feasibility of forming successful global teams. Depending on the answers to the questions, the assessment identifies areas requiring discussion and resolution.

8. **Executive Leadership Team Meeting Assessment**
   How and Why to Use: Use this assessment with members of the executive team to gauge their satisfaction with their meetings and to determine if meeting time is being spent productively. Use the results with the team to identify changes they want to make.

9. **Executive Leadership Team Assessment**
   How and Why to Use: Use this assessment to evaluate the health of the executive leadership team. Use the issues that are surfaced to help the team develop action plans. Have each member self-evaluate, summarize the results, and share the overall results with the team.

10. **Organization Assessment**
    How and Why to Use: Use this assessment with leaders to quantify their organization's level of readiness for using teams. Each question specifies an area that must be addressed to assure teams can be successful.

TEAM BINGO

We have all experienced meeting new people. Recognizing that these people are now expected to become our teammates, we are interested in finding out about their backgrounds and knowing what each person brings to the team. The first information we need is not really task focused. Spending time finding out personal data sets the foundation for the trust- and relationship-building activities that follow. Depending on the task ahead and what kind of team we are going to become, there is a wide range of activities that can assist in this first step.

The game of bingo, popular throughout the world, can be adapted to have members of a team share personal information about themselves in a nonthreatening and fun manner. The bingo sheet shown can easily be modified to fit the team members and the team task.

Instructions:

1. Distribute a bingo sheet and pencil to each participant.

2. Explain that the task is to *move around* and collect signatures from other participants who say "yes" to the question listed in the box. For example, "Did you play on a sport team in school?" If the answer is "yes," have that person sign the bingo sheet. If "no," say thanks and move to another person.

3. Only one question to a person at a time, then move on to interview other people.

4. It is permitted to go back to a person more than one time.

5. The goal is to be the first person to fill all of the boxes with a signature.

6. Have the winner read through the sheet, reading first the question and then naming which team member said "yes."

7. Congratulate the winner and thank the group for participating.

8. At the end of the activity, ask the team if they were surprised by any of the answers.

9. Conclude by thanking the team for having fun with this, sharing some information, and getting to know each other better. Encourage them to keep finding out about each other in the days ahead.

TEAM BINGO

Did you play on a sport team in school?	Have you worked at the same job for more than five years?	Were you ever a team captain?	Do you have a good singing voice?
Have you lived in more than one country?	Do you have more than one brother or sister?	Are you a good writer?	Do you like to dance?
Do you love or at least like e-mail?	Do you dislike e-mail?	Do you return messages quickly?	Have you ever owned a boat or a motorcycle?
Do you like Mexican and Chinese foods?	Do you have children?	Did you have to share a bedroom with others as a child?	Do you like to cook?

Helpful hints:

- Complete this activity in less than fifteen minutes.

- Play fun, fast-paced music to keep the energy of the team high.

- Have a prize for the first one or two individuals who complete their sheets first.

- As the facilitator, you can sign sheets, too.

- Make the topics general so that someone in the team can honestly say "yes."

- Customize the bingo sheet to make it specific to the audience.

TEAM NORMS

The norms of a team are the shared beliefs regarding what is appropriate behavior for members. Norms define the boundaries of team member behavior, clearly stating what is in-bounds or out-of-bounds. As with the games and sports we play, team members need to know the rules that guide their team. Whenever possible, teams should be involved in developing and agreeing to their norms. Norms allow the team to clarify or define their expectations of one another. They can either help eliminate conflict or provide a structure for dealing with conflict when it does arise.

Instructions:

1. Review the purpose for setting team norms, including the following:

   - Helps maintain consistent behavior among members

   - Clarifies what is acceptable behavior within the team

   - Deals primarily with the behavior affecting the accomplishment of the team's tasks and goals

- Helps the team maintain itself over time

- Encourages each person to make his or her unique contribution to the team

- Defines how team members will treat each other

2. As a team, discuss best and worst team experiences.

3. From past experiences, identify norms that led to good results and list them on a chart.

4. Using the past experiences chart, as a team, select the norm topics important to this team (e.g., how to give feedback, how to address conflict, how work is assigned).

5. Take each topic, draft a norm, and rewrite it until everyone agrees to support it.

6. Propose norms to team leader.

7. Monitor conformance to the norms regularly.

Helpful hints:

- Establish and agree to team norms as soon as possible. If norm setting is delayed, norms tend to focus on correcting negative behaviors.

- If possible, have norms that describe desired behaviors instead of norms that describe behaviors that should be avoided.

- When appropriate, involve the leader/manager in establishing norms or have the leader/manager kickoff and sanction the process.

- Set up processes for monitoring norms and for addressing non-conformance.

- Provide the group with examples of norms to use as idea starters.

- Have norms for how meetings will be conducted as well as regarding the overall functioning of the team.

MEETING TOOLS

If you must spend your time in meetings, make the most of them! No matter what type of team you are on, some amount of the work of the team is spent in meetings. The following tools and ideas can be customized to fit your team's needs to solve problems and correct the causes of ineffective meetings.

Instructions:

1. Carefully read each of the meeting tools on the following pages.

2. Identify the one(s) that could benefit your team most.

3. Modify the forms to reflect the meeting or your team's needs.

4. Administer the tool either before or during a meeting.

5. Score the results.

6. Facilitate a discussion and action-planning session based on the results.

Helpful hints:

- Carefully use these tools. Used selectively, they can provide information in an effective manner. Overused, they lose effectiveness and credibility.

- Never use a tool to gather information unless you are 100 percent certain you will use the results to bring about change.

Team Meeting Assessment

1. How often are we following our agreed-to norms?

1	2	3	4	5	6	7	8	9	10
Never		Rarely		Sometimes		Usually		Always	

2. How do you rate the overall quality and results of our discussions?

1	2	3	4	5	6	7	8	9	10
Poor		Low		Satisfactory		High	Outstanding		

3. How often does the information presented add value to our meeting?

1	2	3	4	5	6	7	8	9	10
Never		Rarely		Sometimes		Usually		Always	

4. When are the correct topics getting on the agenda?

1	2	3	4	5	6	7	8	9	10
Never		Rarely		Sometimes		Usually		Always	

5. How often are we spending an appropriate amount of time on the agenda topics?

1	2	3	4	5	6	7	8	9	10
Never		Rarely		Sometimes		Usually		Always	

MEETING NORMS—SOME SUGGESTIONS

- Set the agenda and communicate it prior to the meeting.
- Start the meeting on time.
- Make sure only one person talks at a time.
- Focus on the current topic.
- Be flexible to others' ideas.
- Listen openly and avoid defensive responses.
- Respect others.
- Express your opinions.
- Agree to disagree.
- Stay involved in the meeting discussions.
- Avoid repeating points that you agree with.
- Celebrate progress and wins.
- End the meeting on time or agree to extend the time.
- End the meeting as friends.

This Facilitator Skills Checklist can be used for self-evaluation or second-party evaluation.

Meeting Facilitator Skills Checklist

		Strong	Okay	Weak
1.	Describes the goals, objectives, or purpose of the meeting	____	____	____
2.	Has, and sticks to, an agenda	____	____	____
3.	States problems and objectives clearly	____	____	____
4.	Sells ideas and alternatives	____	____	____
5.	Builds and maintains enthusiasm	____	____	____
6.	Requests feedback	____	____	____
7.	Admits mistakes	____	____	____
8.	Assists group in identifying next steps or actions needed	____	____	____
9.	Reads the group accurately	____	____	____
10.	Listens and encourages others to listen attentively	____	____	____
11.	Deals effectively with anger or conflict	____	____	____
12.	Builds trust and openness	____	____	____
13.	Encourages others to give more information	____	____	____
14.	Presents one's biases openly and honestly	____	____	____
15.	Explains information clearly and accurately	____	____	____
16.	Clarifies issues effectively and brings them to closure	____	____	____
17.	Asks frequent questions to involve everyone	____	____	____
18.	Encourages new ideas and creative solutions	____	____	____
19.	Clarifies or resolves any misunderstandings	____	____	____
20.	Follows up and supports the group	____	____	____
21.	Helps others solve problems constructively	____	____	____

Meeting Facilitator Skills Checklist

	Strong	Okay	Weak
22. Acknowledges or rewards "a job well done"	___	___	___
23. Asks for help and involvement	___	___	___
24. Stays involved in the process rather than the content	___	___	___
25. Listens to all discussion before asking for a decision	___	___	___
26. Summarizes key points and agreements	___	___	___
27. Identifies next steps and actions	___	___	___
28. Avoids a condescending tone of voice	___	___	___

The next two forms provide a framework for soliciting meeting feedback from the facilitator and the meeting participants. The third form is an action-planning template.

Meeting Feedback Checklist

Group _____

Date _____

	Yes	Partially	No
Was there a clear agenda?	___	___	___
Were there clear objectives?	___	___	___
Was the agenda followed?	___	___	___
Did each member participate?	___	___	___
Did the meeting start on time?			
Did the meeting end on time or end early?	___	___	___
Was the meeting facilitated and led effectively?	___	___	___
Was the meeting summarized?	___	___	___
Were opportunities, rather than problems, identified?	___	___	___
Were expectations, roles, and responsibilities clear?	___	___	___
Were specific tasks established when needed?	___	___	___
Were follow-up tasks established when needed?	___	___	___
Were commitments asked for and made when needed?	___	___	___
Did the facilitator explain why, as well as what was to be done?	___	___	___
Did the facilitator react appropriately to nonverbal communication?	___	___	___
Was paraphrasing used for clarification or summarizing?	___	___	___
Were problems phrased as "how-to" opportunities?	___	___	___
Was active listening used?			
Was the facilitator a positive role model?	___	___	___
Was the time and place of the next meeting established (if necessary)?	___	___	___
Were headlines used? "Bottom-line" statements? (state point and elaborate)	___	___	___
Overall, did the meeting meet or exceed your expectations?	___	___	___

Meeting Participant Checklist

Team, Department, or Organization _____

Date _____

	Yes	Partially	No
Did we all show up on time so the meeting could start when planned?	___	___	___
Did we participate in a positive fashion?	___	___	___
Were we prepared?	___	___	___
Did we listen to others?	___	___	___
Did we phrase problems as "how-to" opportunities?	___	___	___
Did we use paraphrasing and questions to ensure understanding?	___	___	___
Did we give and accept feedback constructively?	___	___	___
Did we avoid negative prejudgments such as "nothing can be done"?	___	___	___
Did we talk about the present and avoid dwelling negatively on the past?	___	___	___
Did we make suggestions and actively problem solve?	___	___	___
Did we support change?	___	___	___
Did we respect the opinions of other participants?	___	___	___
Did we avoid assumptions and deal with facts?	___	___	___
Did we allow the facilitator to guide the meeting when needed?	___	___	___

Action Planning for Meetings

What Action? _____

_____

_____

Responsible Person: _____

Start Date: _____

Follow-up Date: _____

End Date: _____

Completion Date: _____

Resources Needed: _____

_____

Comments: _____

_____

_____

_____

_____

_____

_____

_____

THE TRIPLEWIN RELATIONSHIP ASSESSMENT

TripleWin Relationship Continuum

Compete · Coexist · Coordinate · Collaborate

Win-Lose · Win-Win

©TripleWin Consulting LLC, used with permission.

This relationship continuum depicts a range of win-lose to win-win relationships. In all relationships, people move back and forth along the scale, depending on the situation and the people involved. Conflict occurs all along the continuum. On the right, conflict is used *positively* to solve problems. On the left, conflict is used *negatively* to inflict damage. There is no magic step that moves an individual or group from win-lose to win-win. It takes conscious attention and continuous effort. However, team behaviors and processes work best in a win-win environment.

Instructions:

1. Present the TripleWin Relationship Continuum using the information found in chapter 1.

2. Facilitate a discussion about the behaviors exhibited in a win-lose and in a win-win environment.

3. Discuss the costs and benefits for this team based on where they fall on this continuum.

4. Hand out a copy of the assessment (or complete before the session and share results in this meeting).

5. Based on results, discuss changes the team members must make to improve their relationships.

Helpful hints:

- Use this continuum only after the team is familiar with the language and agrees with collaboration as their goal.

- Consider introducing and discussing the continuum in one session, conducting the assessment at another, and presenting results at a third session.

- Allow for anonymity to increase honesty.

- Use this instrument to establish a baseline that can monitor a team's progress.

- This instrument is helpful after a team has experience and history working together.

TripleWin Relationship Assessment

Instructions: *Circle the number that most closely corresponds to where your team falls along the continuum. Upon completion, total all your responses and place the total in the box provided.*

1. When we disagree on an issue that is important to each of us, which of these stages most accurately represents how we behave toward one another?

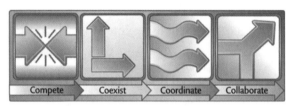

Compete ❯ Coexist ❯ Coordinate ❯ Collaborate

©TripleWin Consulting LLC, used with permission.

Compete	Coexist	Coordinate	Collaborate
1 2	3	4	5 6

2. How open and honest are we with each other? Do we encourage open discussion within the team?

1   2   3   4   5   6

Very guarded   Open and honest

3. Do we treat each other with respect by not using sarcasm and jokes that may hurt one another?

1   2   3   4   5   6

Sarcastic and hurtful   Respectful

4. Do we treat each other with understanding by giving one another the benefit of the doubt and seeking to understand each other before making judgments?

1   2   3   4   5   6

Judgmental   Understanding

TripleWin Relationship Assessment

5. Do we support one another, celebrating each others' successes, helping each other when problems occur, and sharing our skills and talents so we can all grow together?

| 1 | 2 | 3 | 4 | 5 | 6 |

Independent   Supportive

6. Do we take the time to get to know each other—not only concerning work issues, but also personal issues?

| 1 | 2 | 3 | 4 | 5 | 6 |

Do not take time to develop   Take time to develop
relationships   relationships

7. Do we behave in a trustworthy manner, safeguarding confidential information and keeping our commitments to one another?

| 1 | 2 | 3 | 4 | 5 | 6 |

Not trustworthy or reliable   Trustworthy and reliable

8. Do we work together to resolve conflicts openly, or do we ignore or avoid issues?

| 1 | 2 | 3 | 4 | 5 | 6 |

Ignore or avoid the issues   Openly resolve conflicts

TOTAL

TripleWin Relationship Assessment Scoring

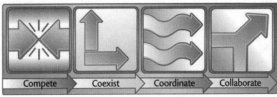

©TripleWin Consulting LLC, used with permission.

| 8 through 17 | 18 through 27 | 28 through 37 | 38 through 48 |
| **Competitive** | **Coexisting** | **Coordinating** | **Collaborating** |

TRUST CONTINUUM

Trust is the basis of human relationships and does not always come naturally. People must want it and work for it. Trust can be difficult to achieve. Without trust, rules and guidelines can keep a group on course but may keep a true team spirit from forming. Time and positive experiences build trust and loosen up boundaries and remove restrictions. Mistakes and deceit can destroy trust. Once built, trust can allow a relationship to weather a storm. People who trust each other accept differences. Once broken, trust is difficult to put back into place. The following personal characteristics, attitudes, and behaviors contribute to a climate of either trust of distrust.[1]

Trust-Building Characteristics & Attitudes	Mistrust-Building Characteristics & Attitudes
Open	Closed
Supportive	Controlling
Willing to risk	Unwilling to risk
Respectful	Disrespectful
Genuine	Hypocritical
Cooperative	Competitive
Mutual	Superior
Problem centered	Solution minded
Accepting and warm	Rejecting and cold
Dependable	Unpredictable
Expert	Inept
Accountable	Unaccountable

1. Chartier, "Trust-Orientation Profile," 135-142.

Instructions:

1. As a team, discuss the importance of trust between team members.

2. Review the "trust/distrust list" and ensure understanding of all the characteristics and attitudes.

3. Pass out a several copies to each participant of the trust/distrust list constructed as a continuum.

4. Have the team split into pairs and find quiet places to talk.

5. The first step is to individually mark each of the items along the continuum based on your current relationship with the other member of your pair.

6. Taking turns, as a pair, discuss what has caused the trust or distrust, being specific.

7. Together, identify ways to increase the level of trust in the relationship. Agree to work on at least one specific step.

8. Have all the pairs change and conduct the activity as many times as possible.

9. After the pair activity, have a final discussion as a team to identify the five things the team can do to increase trust within the team.

Helpful hints:

- Do not use this activity in high-conflict situations with a team that cannot honestly discuss feelings and behaviors in a constructive manner.

- Monitor the pairs and assist if necessary.

- Pair people up who will most benefit from the dialogue.

PASSING THE BATON—CHANGING LEADERS

A team's performance is connected to its leader. When a team leader changes, a process for quickly assimilating the new leader helps avoid performance setbacks due to this significant change. Taken from the practice used in relay races, passing the baton from one leader to another can set up the new leader for success while allowing closure for the departing leader and a new beginning for the team. At a minimum, discussion about the leader, the team, and the work ahead of the team begins with this process.

Instructions:

1. Ask a facilitator (nonteam member) to meet with both the departing and the new, incoming leader to clarify the objectives of the session and to coach both leaders on their roles. This can be done with each leader separately or together. (15 minutes)

2. Have the total team meet. The departing team leader should talk about: (15 minutes)

   • What the leader feels best about (personally, accomplishments of the team, what he or she has learned)

   • What the leader feels are the team's strengths

   • What the leader feels are the biggest challenges facing the team

   • What the leader would focus on if he or she were staying

3. The team should thank the departing leader. (10 minutes)

4. Both departing and incoming leader should leave the room. Then the team should list on a piece of chart paper the following information: (20 minutes)

   • Questions they have about their new team leader (leadership style, priorities, etc.)

- What they would like their new team leader to know about the team

- Their expectations, how they work together, how they make decisions, how they communicate, how they we solve problems

- Hot or key issues they want the new team leader to know about (e.g., unresolved issues, challenges facing the team

5. The new leader should then rejoin the team, and the facilitator should lead the team through a discussion of each of the areas listed above, beginning with having the new leader share information about himself or herself based on the team's list. (45 minutes)

6. The new leader should tell the team what they can expect. (10 minutes)

7. The team should end the session by reconfirming their team norms and identifying topics that need additional discussion. (15 minutes)

8. Periodic reviews should be conducted to monitor progress and the success of the team's performance.

Helpful hints:

- Schedule the session before the new leader begins to work with the team and before the departing leader is gone.

- Schedule the length of the meeting to allow enough time for a quality discussion to occur.

- Conduct this session in a quiet environment.

- Encourage group dialogue that maintains a constructive tone.

- Involve the departing team leader in the first part of the session but not in the second half of the session.

- Use a facilitator until the team is able to facilitate the session with care and consideration.

ASSIMILATING NEW TEAM MEMBERS

For a team to maintain its effectiveness and performance over an extended period of time, the team must have an effective process for changing team members. The goal of this activity is to assimilate or integrate new members into an existing team by introducing the team to the new members and the new members to the team in a manner that sets everyone up for success. A guaranteed outcome is that the new members learn the culture and norms of the team before trying to work as a member on the team.

Instructions:

1. A facilitator (nonteam member) should meet with the new team members to clarify the objectives of the session and to coach the new members on their role. (15 minutes)

2. Then the total team should meet. Each new team member should talk for about 5 to 7 minutes about the following:

   - Personal background (name, past job roles, brief work and personal history, hobbies or interests, how he or she came to work at this organization)

   - What skills he or she brings to the team; what the new team member has have to offer the team; strengths and weaknesses of the new team member

   - What the new team member needs in return from the team

3. New members should then leave the room. The team should list on a piece of chart paper the following information: (20 minutes)

   - Other things they would like to know about their new team members

   - What they would like their new team members to know about the team

   - Their expectations, how they work together, how they make decisions, how they communicate, how they solve problems

   - Hot or key issues they want new team members to know about (e.g., unresolved issues, challenges facing the team)

4. The new members should then rejoin the team, and the facilitator should lead the team through a discussion of each of the areas listed above. (30–45 minutes)

5. The new team members should take turns telling the team what it can expect from them. (10 minutes)

6. Existing team members, individually or collectively, should tell what the new members can expect in return. (5 minutes)

7. The team should end the session by reviewing and confirming the team norms and by clarifying all team members' assignments, roles, and responsibilities. (15 minutes)

8. Ongoing discussions should be held to monitor progress and success of the team's performance.

Helpful hints:

- Schedule the session before the new team members begin to work on the team.

- Schedule the length of meeting to allow enough time for a quality discussion to occur.

- Conduct this session in a quiet environment.

- Encourage group dialogue that maintains a constructive tone.

- Involve the existing team leader as one of the existing members of the team.

- Use a facilitator until the team is able to facilitate the session with care and consideration.

CONTINUOUS IMPROVEMENT AT WARP SPEED

All organizations strive for continuous improvement in how they produce their products or provide their services. At times, the team members need to be convinced that there are better ways to do things. The following activity and discussion can increase the team's energy to strive for breakthrough results. The activity is called "Warp Speed" in reference to the speed jets achieve.

Instructions:

1. Collect the following materials before conducting the event: one small ball, a stopwatch or digital watch, and a tablet and marking pen for capturing team results.

2. Ask everyone to stand in a circle.

3. Review the three rules to Warp Speed:

   - The ball must start and stop with the facilitator.

   - Everyone must touch the ball only once.

- The team establishes a sequence by their throws that, once established, becomes the sequence that must be repeated in all rounds of the activity.

4. Review the activity setup:

   - The facilitator throws the ball to someone in the circle.

   - Ask that person to throw the ball to another person on the other side of the circle.

   - This throwing and catching continues until everyone in the circle has both thrown and caught the ball *one* time.

   - No planning is allowed in this first round of establishing the sequence.

   - It is okay to talk during all phases of this activity.

5. Once the sequence has been established, ask participants to throw the ball through the established sequenced while being timed to establish the base time.

6. Time the sequence using a stopwatch or digital watch.

7. Establish the team's initial time.

8. Offer the team 2 to 3 minutes to redesign their process to improve their time, reminding them that they must adhere to the three rules.

9. After each timed round, ask the team the following questions. Did the ball start and stop with the facilitator? Did you each touch it once? In the right sequence? If the rules have been met, record the time on the tablet and calculate the improvement.

10. Offer the team another 2 to 3 minutes to improve their process to significantly decrease their time.

11. Finish the final round when the team has accomplished significant time reductions as compared to its initial time.

12. After this activity, ask the team to identify 5 things it can do to increase the team's effectiveness in achieving breakthrough results in the daily work environment.

13. Ask the team to determine what support it needs to make these changes.

Helpful hints:

- Limit the number of rounds to five or less.

- A signal, worked out in advance, helps the team establish a sequence. For example, have everyone put their hands behind their back after they have finished their turn of catching and throwing the ball.

- Emphasize that is it important to remember where the ball came from and where to throw it next.

- The event facilitator should stay out of the strategizing sessions and should not give any advice.

- Do not answer too many questions; just restate the three rules.

- Most teams of 24 participants can complete the task in less than 5 seconds; smaller teams can complete the task in under 2 seconds.

- Decide on how far to encourage the team to go (e.g., teams that are working well can be encouraged to go farther than teams experiencing significant frustrations).

- Discuss the learning points after the event with the following questions:

  What helped us be successful?

  How was our quality?

  Did we listen to everyone?

  How well did we do?

  How can we bring this same energy and results to our workplace?

ASSESSMENTS

Assessments are included in many of the chapters of *The Driving Force*. They are important and useful tools when working with teams. Used correctly, assessments can pinpoint an area requiring attention or can highlight a team's strength. They also provide insight and knowledge to people about themselves and the way their team functions. These assessments were created to address the needs of a specific type of team. They can be modified to fit other audiences as well. The key success factor is to use the data the assessments provide. Use them to gain insight or to identify changes that need to be made.

We have reprinted the assessments in the toolkit for your convenience. Combined with the other activities outlined in the toolkit, these assessments provide you with the means to help your teams improve their performance and increase their understanding of how teams work.

Organizational Readiness Assessment: Are You Ready to Use Teams?

Directions: *This assessment is to be used to describe your organization using the listed organization practices as a guide. For each of the statements that follow, answer "yes" or "no."*

1. Are the organization's values aligned with implementing a team concept?

2. Do we pay attention to the organizational roadblocks that can interfere with the early success of teams?

3. Have we planned for changes and developed change strategies and skills?

4. Have we examined past change efforts, both successes and failures, and generated ideas to make sure this change initiative works?

5. Because teams are made up of people with their own individual needs and wants, are we prepared to address our team members' primary issues and concerns?

6. Will the team structure integrate into our daily operations?

7. Did we clearly link the team's purpose to the overall organization purpose?

8. Are the various teams connected together to assure alignment throughout the organization?

9. Can we provide clear, ongoing direction to the teams?

10. Have we comprehended the role of the managers in relation to the teams, and do we have a plan to train, reinforce, and continue to work with the managers in their new responsibilities?

11. Are sufficient funds and resources allocated to sustain the team effort once it is launched?

12. Is a method in place to hold teams accountable for a return on the investment?

Organizational Readiness Assessment: Are You Ready to Use Teams?

Scoring

This Organizational Readiness Assessment can be completed by individual leaders and anonymously tallied. Another option is to have the key leadership group share their assessments to reach agreements about areas needing improvement and to identify next steps. Totaling the number of "yes" answers quantifies the overall level of readiness.

9-12 The organization has many of the characteristics required to support teams in place. Continue to monitor once teams are operational and reinforce effective practices.

5-8 Some of the key characteristics are in place, while others are missing. Teams are at risk in more than half of the required areas. Build on the organization's strengths, while addressing the missing areas. Teams are at some risk. For any "no" answers, develop an action item to address the shortfall.

0-4 Most or all of the characteristics are missing. Evaluate the potential for improvement, and establish a comprehensive development plan. If changes cannot be made, do not launch the team. For any "no" answers, develop an action item to address the shortfall.

Great Team Player Characteristics

Directions: *Read the following eleven characteristics, and rate yourself for how you act on* **this** *team.*

1 = poor   2 = okay   3 = great

_____ I communicate my feelings, opinions, thoughts, and ideas openly.

_____ I appreciate the skills of other team members.

_____ I help make well-informed decisions.

_____ I put the organization and team before my own goals.

_____ I help develop other team members.

_____ I honor the different opinions and characteristics of others.

_____ I care about other team members.

_____ I involve other team members appropriately.

_____ I build on the ideas of others.

_____ I do my share of the work.

_____ I listen to others.

Scoring

11-16   Room to make major changes. Your performance may be keeping the team from reaching high performance. Build on any "2's" or "3's" but select at least one of the items you marked with a "1" and make a serious effort to improve.

17-22   Identify items with a "1" rating and focus on improving your performance. Other team members may focus on your weaknesses versus your strengths unless they see you working on the low-scored items.

23-33   You are a good example to others. Keep improving your own performance while helping others work on improving their team behaviors.

Team Effectiveness Assessment

Directions: *This assessment is to be used to describe your team using the listed characteristics. For each statement that follows, refer to the scale provided and decide which number corresponds to your level of agreement with the statement; then write that number in the blank to the left of the statement.*

1 = rarely   2 = sometimes   3 = often   4 = usually   5 = almost always

_____ We have shared and flexible leadership roles.

_____ We have individual and mutual accountability.

_____ Our interdependent tasks and relationships are well understood.

_____ We use measures that accurately track our performance.

_____ We have open discussions and disclose all relevant information.

_____ We use a collaborative problem-solving approach.

_____ Our focus is on the production of actual products or services.

_____ We have a shared commitment to our team goals.

_____ Every team member's unique talents and knowledge is fully utilized.

_____ We handle conflict in a constructive and direct manner.

_____ Everyone actively participates in decision making.

_____ We have agreed to established work procedures, and we follow them.

_____ We have a strong group identity and perceive ourselves as a team.

_____ We encourage reasonable experimentation, innovation, and creativity.

_____ We maintain honest, trusting relationships.

Team Effectiveness Assessment

Scoring

The Team Effectiveness Assessment can be completed by each individual team member and tallied anonymously. Another option is to have team members share their assessments with the team at a team-building meeting to reach agreements about areas needing improvement and to identify next steps.

50-75   The team has many of the characteristics for high performance teamwork in place. Continue to monitor progress and reinforce effective practices.

25-49   Some of the key characteristics are in place, but others are missing. Build on the team's strengths, while addressing the low scoring characteristics.

15-24   Most of the necessary characteristics are missing. Evaluate the potential for improvement, and establish a comprehensive development plan. If changes cannot be made, consider disbanding the team.

Project Team Readiness Assessment

Directions: *This assessment is to be used to describe your organization using the listed characteristics. For each of the statements that follow, answer "yes" or "no." For any "no" answer, develop an action item to address the shortfall.*

1. Have all of the right project team members been identified, recruited, and assigned to the task?
2. Are the project team members motivated to perform the task at hand?
3. Has a clear problem definition been written?
4. Has the problem-solving process that best matches the task been identified?
5. Do the project team members have adequate group and meeting skills?
6. Is a plan in place to train the project team?
7. Is a plan in place to assure ongoing leadership support?
8. Has a well-defined timeline been developed?
9. Have necessary approvals been obtained to ensure that the project team has access to necessary information and resources?
10. Have external resources, such as consultants or facilitators, been hired to guide the process?

Virtual Team Attributes Self-Assessment

Instructions: *Check the boxes of the attributes you consistently demonstrate.*

❏ I enjoy communicating through e-mail.

❏ I am a self-starter.

❏ I like to work on projects independently.

❏ I enjoy talking on the telephone.

❏ I enjoy writing down my ideas, plans, and projects.

❏ I prefer having my own projects.

❏ I solve problems effectively on my own without input, information, and clarification from others.

❏ I enjoy learning new things on the computer.

❏ I am well organized.

❏ I like to plan my own work.

❏ It is easy for me to ask for help and input.

❏ I thrive on solving problems that arise unexpectedly.

❏ I am comfortable defining and clarifying my roles and responsibilities.

❏ I take the time to inform others about critical information about my activities.

❏ I enjoy building on the ideas of others.

❏ I am good at clarifying others' statements to understand their points of view.

❏ I like having well-established procedures and policies.

❏ I like structuring my own work schedule.

❏ I am able to solve computer problems myself.

❏ I prefer working with minimal direction.

❏ I like contributing to a team's efforts.

❏ I value feedback and ideas from others.

Total of checked boxes _____

Virtual Team Attributes Self-Assessment

Scoring

0-7   Only a few attributes were selected that are found in suc-
        cessful virtual team members; therefore, there is a low
        probability of success as a virtual team member.

8-15   Some attributes were selected that are found in success-
        ful virtual team members; this team member may require
        additional training or support to succeed as part of a vir-
        tual team.

16-22   Many attributes were selected that are found in success-
        ful virtual team members; therefore, there is a high prob-
        ability of success as a virtual team member.

Quick-Change Team Assessment

Directions: *Use the following checklist to determine your level of readiness to be a member of a quick-change team. Put a checkmark next to the items you feel you have mastered. Consider developing the items not mastered to future assist you in becoming a skilled quick-change team member.*

❑ I enjoy new experiences and people.

❑ I meet new people easily.

❑ I build trusting relationships easily.

❑ I request feedback on my behavior and performance.

❑ I follow meeting agenda and processes.

❑ I state problems clearly.

❑ I sell my ideas and alternatives.

❑ I admit mistakes.

❑ I assist others in identifying next steps.

❑ I listen attentively to others.

❑ I encourage others to share their ideas.

❑ I deal effectively with my anger and frustration.

❑ I explain information clearly and accurately.

❑ I clarify issues effectively.

❑ I ask questions frequently.

❑ I encourage new ideas, suggestions, and methods.

❑ I resolve misunderstandings.

❑ I implement decisions.

❑ I help others when they need it.

❑ I ask for help when I need it.

❑ I remain open to new people and their opinions.

❑ I work independently.

❑ I work interdependently.

❑ I accept direction from others.

❑ I follow through on my commitments.

❑ I tackle challenges with a positive attitude and approach.

Global Team Feasibility Assessment

Directions: Read each of the following questions and answer "yes" or "no." If the answer is "yes," describe what is in place that assures this item will not be a problem for the global team. If the answer is "no," determine if that item provides sufficient doubt for moving forward with forming a global team.

1. Are the top leaders from all countries fully supportive of this global team?
2. Can every country affected by this work be involved in the team?
3. Is the organization motivated to work on this task?
4. Can training and time bridge the cultural differences and result in true teamwork?
5. Can the project criteria be explained in a way that all team members can understand?
6. Is there sufficient funding to allow for travel and face-to-face sessions to build the team?
7. Are there clear deliverables and timelines to guide the team's work?
8. Has a team leader been identified who can guide this team's work?
9. Can a common language be spoken?
10. Can process resources be allocated to develop the team and assist in establishing effective team practices?

Scoring

Count the "yes" and "no" scores for each question from each decision-maker. For any item with "no" answers, discuss the item and reach agreement on whether or not it is sufficient reason to *not* form a global team.

Executive Leadership Team Meeting Assessment

Directions: *For periodic review of meeting effectiveness, have each member complete the following assessment.*

1. How often do we stay on track with the agenda, including time for each item?

1	2	3	4	5	6	7	8	9	10

Never Rarely Sometimes Usually Always

Comments:

2. How often is the overall quality of our discussions high?

1	2	3	4	5	6	7	8	9	10

Never Rarely Sometimes Usually Always

Comments:

3. Would you rate the overall quality of information presented as high?

1	2	3	4	5	6	7	8	9	10

Never Rarely Sometimes Usually Always

Comments:

4. How often are the correct topics getting on the agenda?

1	2	3	4	5	6	7	8	9	10

Never Rarely Sometimes Usually Always

Comments:

5. Do we spend an appropriate amount of time on agenda items?

1	2	3	4	5	6	7	8	9	10

Never Rarely Sometimes Usually Always

Comments:

Executive Leadership Team Assessment

Directions: *To evaluate your executive leadership team's health, complete the following assessment by circling the number that most accurately describes typical team meetings or problem-solving sessions. Total the numbers circled and refer to the scoring information for a general assessment of your team's health.*

1. Decision Making

1   2   3   4   5

Process is undefined; top leader makes most of the decisions.

Well-defined process, with high level of involvement by members.

2. Meeting Format

1   2   3   4   5

Meetings are focused on presentations, and discussions are polite and orderly.

Dialogue and debate create high energy and raise new issues.

3. Conflict

1   2   3   4   5

Conflict is discouraged and handled one-on-one, not during the team meeting.

Conflict is used to stimulate discussion of key topics during the team meeting.

4. Relationships

1   2   3   4   5

Win-lose relationships are allowed to exist; inappropriate behavior goes unaddressed.

Win-win relationships are developed and nurtured by spending time building trust.

5. Accountability

1   2   3   4   5

Little to no follow-up or review of decisions or actions is completed.

Decisions and action steps are monitored and tracked.

Executive Leadership Team Assessment

6. Strategy

1	2	3	4	5

Strategy is limited to annual business plan discussions and when new situations require it.

Strategic items are discussed on a regular basis as the primary team and meeting focus.

7. Top Leader

1	2	3	4	5

Top leader sets the tone as his/her meeting and usually talks first and most often in key discussions.

Leadership and accountability are shared; top leader models effective team member behaviors.

8. Balanced Participation

1	2	3	4	5

Top leader and a few other members control the discussion and drive decisions and actions.

Every person on the team plays an active part and makes a meaningful contribution.

Scoring

8-16   Little or no structure is in place for an executive leadership team. Some structure exists to function as a committee or staff of the top executive. Evaluate the need for teamwork and make necessary changes to create a team environment or accept the role of executive committee.

17-25   Some structure for an executive leadership team is in place. Areas with scores of 2 or below must be addressed to reach high performance while building on areas that score 3 and above. With additional effort, an effective executive leadership team can be built.

26-40   Most of the structure for high performance is in place. Monitoring actual results and maintaining the right relationships are critical to sustain a high level of teamwork. Assimilate new team members to avoid regression. Any score below 3 needs to be examined and addressed.

Organization Assessment

Directions: *For each of the strategies listed below, circle the word(s) that best describe how much this particular strategy is in place within your organization today.*

1. Shared and flexible leadership roles

Not At All   Somewhat   Totally

2. Individual and mutual accountability

Not At All   Somewhat   Totally

3. Interrelated performance measures

Not At All   Somewhat   Totally

4. Open information sharing

Not At All   Somewhat   Totally

5. Collaborative problem solving

Not At All   Somewhat   Totally

6. Shared commitment to goal(s)

Not At All   Somewhat   Totally

7. Full use of individual members' knowledge

Not At All   Somewhat   Totally

8. Active participation in decision making

Not At All   Somewhat   Totally

9. Experimentation, innovation, and creativity

Not At All   Somewhat   Totally

10. Honest, trusting relationships

Not At All   Somewhat   Totally

Organization Assessment

Scoring

Each of these strategies plays a key role in supporting teams within an organization. Any item receiving a rating less than "Totally" must be examined to determine if it will be an inhibiting force to the successful use of teams. If it is not possible for the entire organization to implement these strategies, it is essential for the area the team functions in to have these characteristics.

REFERENCES

Beyerlein, M., S. Freedman, C. McGee, and L. Moran. *Beyond Teams: Building the Collaborative Organization*. San Francisco, CA: Jossey-Bass/ Pfeiffer, 2002.

Bridges, William. *Managing Transitions: Making the Most out of Change*. Cambridge, MA: Perseus Books Group, 1991.

Chartier, Myron R. "Trust-Orientation Profile." In *1991 Annual: Developing Human Resource*, 135-142. San Diego, CA: University Associates.

Covey, Stephen R. *The 7 Habits of Highly Effective People: Powerful lessons in personal change*. New York, NY: Simon and Schuster, 1989.

Hackman, Richard. *Groups That Work (and Those That Don't)*. San Francisco, CA: Jossey-Bass Inc., 1990

Hardt, Paul O., and Richard Brynteson. "Swift Virtual Trust." *iBiz Magazine*, December 1998.

Hersey, Paul. *Situational Leadership*, New York, NY: Warner Books Inc., 1984.

Jones, Patricia, and Larry Kahaner. *Say It and Live It, The 50 Corporate Mission Statements That Hit The Mark*. New York, NY: Currency Doubleday, 1995.

Klatt, B., S. Murphy, and D. Irvine. *Accountability: Practical Tools for Focusing on Clarity, Commitment and Results*. London: Kogan Page Limited, 1997.

Katzenbach, Jon R., and Douglas K. Smith. *The Wisdom of Teams: Creating the High-Performance Organization*. Boston, MA: Harvard Business School Press, 1993.

Kriegel, Robert, and David Brandt. *Sacred Cows Make the Best Burgers.* New York, NY: Warner Books Inc., 1996.

Larson, Carl E., and Frank M. J. LaDasto. *Teamwork: What Must Go Right/ What Can Go Wrong.* Beverly Hills, CA: Sage Publications, Inc., 1989.

Lawler III, Edward E. *High-Involvement Management: Participative Strategies for Improving Organizational Performance.* San Francisco, CA: Jossey-Bass, 1986.

LeFauve, Richard G., and Arnoldo C. Hax. "Managerial and Technological Innovations at Saturn Corporation." In *MIT Management*, 8-19. Cambridge, MA: MIT Sloan School of Management, Spring 1992.

Lipnack, Jessica, and Jeffrey Stamps. *Virtual Teams: Reaching Across Space, Time and Organizations with Technology.* New York, NY: John Wiley & Sons, 1997.

McShane, Steven L., and Mary Ann Von Glinow. *Organizational Behavior: Emerging Realities for the Workplace Revolution.* New York: McGraw-Hill, 2000.

Morgan, Eileen. *Navigating Cross-Cultural Ethics: What Global Managers Do Right to Keep from Going Wrong.* Woburn, MA: Butterworth-Heinemann, 1998.

O'Toole, Jack. *Forming the Future: Lessons from the Saturn Corporation.* Cambridge, MA: Blackwell Publishers, 1996.

Tuckman, B. W. "Developmental Sequence in Small Groups," In *Psychological Bulletin*, vol. 63, 1965, 384-399.

Weisbord, Marvin R. *Productive Workplaces.* San Francisco, CA: Jossey-Bass, 1989.

Ulrich, Dave, Steve Kerr, and Ron Ashkenas. *The G.E. Work-Out: How to Implement GE's Revolutionary Method for Busting Bureaucracy and Attacking Organizational Problems—Fast!* New York, NY: McGraw-Hill, 2002.

INDEX